THE CHURCH AND BOYS

The Bible Reading Fellowship
15 The Chambers, Vineyard
Abingdon OX14 3FE
brf.org.uk

The Bible Reading Fellowship (BRF) is a Registered Charity (233280)

ISBN 978 0 85746 509 2
First published 2016
10 9 8 7 6 5 4 3 2 1 0
All rights reserved

Cover images: Front © Oliver Rossi/Corbis; Back © Vanesa Munoz/Trevillion Images

Acknowledgements
Unless otherwise stated, scripture quotations are taken from The Holy Bible, New International
Version (Anglicised edition) copyright © 1979, 1984, 2011 by Biblica. Used by permission of
Hodder & Stoughton Publishers, an Hachette UK company. All rights reserved. 'NIV' is a registered
trademark of Biblica. UK trademark number 1448790.

Every effort has been made to trace and contact copyright owners for material used in this
resource. We apologise for any inadvertent omissions or errors, and would ask those concerned to
contact us so that full acknowledgement can be made in the future.

A catalogue record for this book is available from the British Library

Printed and bound by CPI Group (UK) Ltd, Croydon CR0 4YY

THE
CHURCH
AND BOYS
MAKING THE CONNECTION

NICK HARDING

CONTENTS

Introduction

Since writing my Grove booklet *Boys, God and the Church* (Grove, 2007) on the subject of boys and the church, which forms the basis of some of the thinking behind this resource, I have become increasingly aware that there is a problem that's simply not going away: the church is not always an ideal place for boys to be, to grow and to thrive. I have had hundreds of conversations and email exchanges with church group leaders, parents and Christian leaders who see that there's a problem but don't know what to do about it. Is it 'just them?' they ask.

Having been raised in a 'Christian home' many years ago, I was in the habit of attending church, and I benefited greatly from an all-male Boys' Brigade that taught me and helped me in ways that have become apparent only as I have grown older. But in church itself, and particularly the main morning services, I can still remember being bewildered by the ladies who wore hats, the flower arrangements, and some of the new songs—or 'choruses', as they were then known—that seemed just a little wet!

I work with a great many churches and, despite a few exceptions, the majority of children engaged in church activities, whether that's Messy Church or Sunday groups, are girls. Peter Brierley has researched church trends for many years. *Reaching and Keeping Tweenagers* (Christian Research, 2002) identifies that girls are more likely to go to church than boys. Looking at adult gender trends in *Religious*

Trends (2005), he suggests that, at the current rate, men will be a rare sight in the church by 2028. Boys are not going to church in great numbers, and men are not, either.

The ideas and suggestions in this book are principally about working with boys aged around four through to about eleven. Later in the book we look at how we can help boys to move towards manhood. Throughout, there are suggestions for children's groups that will work just as well with youth groups and groups of male teenagers and young men.

The focus is on this age group for three reasons. First, boys learn what it means to be a boy at an early age, and the first few years at nursery and school are key to their development and learning. Second, all the evidence suggests that it is in this age range that boys who do attend church and church-based activities tend to leave because there's not enough to keep them connected. Third, if we can keep boys up to the age of eleven or so, getting them involved and integrated into church life with a vibrant peer group, we are much more likely to keep them through their teenage years. If they form the right habits and learn the right things with the right role models, we will have succeeded and they will have been blessed.

I can do nothing but accept that this book is based on a generalisation! In order to look at gender differences, we have to begin with what comes to our minds as the 'general rule' of what a boy may be like. As you read through the first two chapters and then look at all the practical suggestions, you may well have in mind one or two boys who do not fit the pattern that is assumed. You may also be thinking of a few girls who do fit these descriptions. I know, as a parent of boys and a worker with more than 30 years' experience of children and young people, that not all boys are sporty, not all are into aggressive activities and games, and not all find it difficult to be quiet or sit still without being forced or conditioned to do so. Likewise, not all girls are into things that are pink and fluffy, not all like quiet and arty activities, and not all are compliant and easy to manage. But the majority of boys will be helped by some of the ideas here, and the majority of boys is what this book is concerned with: it's about reaching them, supporting them and keeping them as full and active Christians, contributing effectively to the life of the church. If some or even many of these suggestions work equally well with girls, in mixed groups or in groups that separate boys and girls, then all the better. Try them and see!

There are always exceptions to the rule. Even as things stand (and the same has been true throughout the history of the church), some boys do make it through to adulthood in the church, and many go on to be great evangelists, leaders, and men who give practical support to congregations. The ideas and suggestions collected here offer some hope and assistance to those who want to see a better gender balance in our churches, who want to see boys grow in faith and move towards, as the Boys' Brigade puts it, 'true Christian manliness'.

Where does all this leave girls? I am not advocating that the church should focus on boys at the expense of girls, or should ignore the unique differences that girls bring to a group, to the church and, in time, to church leadership. But I would suggest, without being complacent, that the needs of girls can be and are addressed in other ways within the church. We know that current provisions for children's groups, in terms of ideas and resources and the activities that churches run, are generally more attractive to girls than boys. As we will see later, this may have something to do with the reality that by far the majority of those working with children in a church context are women, who naturally understand the needs of girls well. In terms of 'reaching' girls from the fringes of our church communities, the church does not do a great job, but it is a better job than we do for boys.

There is also something about the physical environment of many churches that may make them more attractive to most girls than to most boys, whether it's the colours, the decorations or the ubiquitous flowers. I recently visited a very modern new-build church where the main worship space had no stained-glass windows, no icons, no banners and no artwork. It had the feel of a secular concert venue— except for the two ornate wrought-iron stands with elaborate flower arrangements that flanked the stage. Not all girls like flowers, but I would venture to suggest that more girls like them than boys do.

There is a place for taking time out with girls and doing activities that are tailored for the needs of most girls, where they can concentrate on those things without the irritation, as they may see it, of having boys around. We will look later at the potential advantages and disadvantages of splitting groups along gender lines, but there can be no harm in setting aside some times when girls can concentrate on the issues that are relevant to them, and boys likewise, separate from each other.

Ultimately, whether doing things together or separately, girls as well as boys can benefit when a little more thought is given to the kind of activities and teaching programmes provided, to meet the gender styles and qualities of both male and female.

CHAPTER 1

WHAT ARE BOYS LIKE?

To recognise that boys are different from girls can be a dangerous thing to do. In this age of right and fair equality, we have to be careful not to reinforce the myths and stereotypes that have kept girls and women subjugated with no excuse for generations. But equality does not mean that we are all the same. In the Church of England, one of the powerful arguments used to support the ordination of women as priests, and latterly as bishops, is that they bring something different to those leadership roles. When we acknowledge that boys are different from girls, and men different from women, we are not saying that either gender is in any way defective or less than God's ideal—far from it.

Boys are different from girls. Boys are part of God's great creation, just as girls are, and God is a God of diversity, but there are a huge number of issues facing boys that make them different and may be affecting the way they become men.

EDUCATION

Much of Western educational theory over the past 50 years has been dominated by the idea that all children are the same. For those working with this theory, 'equal' meant 'identical', and equal opportunities meant there should be no differentiation between genders. For all the right reasons, there were 'glass ceilings' being broken, with girls being encouraged to do games, sports and practical and academic subjects that had been the preserve of the boys, such as engineering, woodwork, football and the sciences. Boys were also encouraged to think more widely about their interests (although it is fair to say that when I was at school there weren't any boys volunteering to play netball). I trained to teach in an era when the daily register was called alphabetically, not divided by gender, and no concessions or adjustments were made to take into account that boys and girls develop and learn in different ways. Much of this was helpful and did no damage, but the underpinning theory made those of us involved in education think that boys and girls were the same in everything, and meant that the same expectations and teaching styles were applied to boys and girls. There was no acknowledgement that 'boys will be boys' and should be allowed to be so.

More recently it has been recognised that if boys and girls are treated the same in the educational world, boys end up performing worse than girls or underachieving. Many projects, papers and research documents have led to a general rethink of the 'total equality' theories and the development of both local and national strategies to help boys learn better and achieve more while in the statutory educational system.

The differences between boys and girls, well documented in some parenting books, including *Raising Boys* by Steve Biddulph (Thorsons, 1998), have a huge impact on the way boys learn best and how they respond spiritually to a relationship with God. We can now acknowledge that their needs are not met by a 'one size fits all' approach.

The church, however, having adopted the view of earlier

educational professionals, has been slow to recognise the differences. Churches still tend to see their children, if they have any, as a homogeneous group who should be treated all the same and, in many cases, tolerated but not relished. So churches have traditionally continued to provide services, clubs, activities, events and camps that treat all children the same, regardless of gender.

NATURE OR NURTURE?

Boys differ from girls in the way they think and behave and in the things they enjoy doing. An obvious example is in the way boys relate to guns. Many parents of boys testify to having worked hard to avoid encouraging their sons to use guns or to play aggressively. Yet very quickly their sons have started playing at shooting each other, perhaps using twigs or their hands as guns. In schools, nurseries and playgroups, boys are encouraged to play with dolls, but those dolls are all too often made into an army or a target for more aggressive behaviours. Much research has gone into working out whether nature or nurture makes boys as they are and as they grow to be, and it seems to be a little of both.

BASIC DEVELOPMENTAL DIFFERENCES

Steve Biddulph identifies several key differences which are important to understand as we consider boys. As babies, boys are less sensitive than girls and less able to recognise individual faces. They are less likely to be able to read expressions or identify what the face is telling them. Boys are much more attached to their mothers as babies but need their fathers more later on. So, in the first few years, bonding with the mother is crucial to the sense of security and safety that boys need, but later that role is taken on by the father. This sets challenges for churches when we consider our lack of male role models and the number of boys we may be working with who have no father-figure to bond with in the home.

BOYS' BRAINS

The brains of boys develop more slowly than those of girls. At birth, the brain is about one-third developed, and growth takes place right up to adolescence. This affects intellectual understanding and memory, and can have an impact on what we call 'maturity'. Testosterone in boys, which becomes more evident as they get older, slows down brain development, whereas oestrogen in girls speeds it up. How, then, can our churches expect ten-year-old boys to behave as sensibly and responsibly as ten-year-old girls? Their brains simply aren't up to it.

Boys' brains have fewer connections between the emotional side and the practical side of the brain. The middle section, where the fibres cross (the corpus callosum), is smaller in boys than in girls. Boys have more internal connections in the right side (practical) of their brains, but the crossover connections are weaker. It is thought that this could explain why more boys than girls have learning difficulties and autism. These brain connections and functions have an influence on men in adulthood, too, with men struggling to describe or connect with the emotional side of their thinking, and taking longer than women to recover from strokes. Often the church looks for both an intellectual level of understanding and an emotional response, which is difficult for boys of any age.

Because of the ways in which boys' brains are wired, they

are generally much less likely to enjoy reading, particularly reading poetry and fiction. Reading involves the 'mechanical' process of identifying the letters, putting them together and having a stab at recognising the words. The next part of the process is to understand the words and what they mean in combination, sentence by sentence and paragraph by paragraph. Understanding demands a degree of empathy and emotional involvement in the text as the reader connects the different parts of the story and imagines how the characters may be feeling.

As boys have more connections in the right side of the brain, boys like practical activities. They are more likely to take things apart, think about how things work, and enjoy factual and evidence-based ideas. This has many advantages, as boys are much more likely to want to think through solutions to problems. The challenge comes for us in churches when we discuss miracles of various sorts in the Bible, as many boys will only consider the practical aspects of the event and decide that, as they can't work out how it happened, it couldn't have happened. For example, boys are likely to think, 'I can't work out the mechanism for how the few loaves and fish became a feast, so it couldn't have happened.' So they may need help in thinking through miracles and responding to God as a consequence. This is tough stuff for boys.

BOYS AND TESTOSTERONE

In the simplest of terms, testosterone makes a boy a boy in the same way as oestrogen makes a girl a girl. Testosterone levels are high before birth, as the male embryo is developing. After birth, the levels drop, and toddlers of both genders tend to behave in similar ways. As boys get older, to around the age of four, testosterone levels rise dramatically and boys become boys. For a year or two, the boy becomes totally absorbed in aggressive and physical activity, loves sport, and behaves very differently from girls of the same age. At that point the differences are embedded.

Testosterone levels increase in boys and men when they win something, succeed, or feel they have done better than others. Testosterone therefore has its natural consequences on the behaviour of boys. They are likely to be aggressive, vie for position and want attention for their successes. They may want to be at the front of the line, the first to be chosen, or the group 'clown' who asks silly questions and makes the group laugh. Boys are likely to push and shove, race around and want to be active. We need to remember that testosterone is a natural part of the make-up of boys as we also work hard in helping them learn to behave appropriately.

Boys will behave in many of these ways to mask the emotional turmoil that they may be going through. Most boys do not wish to be last; they do not want to fail, and they do not want to be compared unfavourably with their male peers. This insecurity comes in part from an awareness that girls are way ahead of them intellectually, so they feel the need to show off in other ways. We cannot condone inappropriate or antisocial behaviour, but we need to remember the biological factors behind it too.

Boys go through growth spurts, rapidly growing out of their clothes, whereas girls tend to grow more gradually. Testosterone will cause boys to have growth spurts when they are aged 11–13, in what Steve Biddulph describes as the period of development when 'the whole nervous system has to rewire itself'. During a growth spurt, a boy's hearing can be affected as their bone and muscle structure within the head changes, so the fact that they struggle to settle and be still, and don't appear to be listening, may not be entirely their fault.

Testosterone is natural but it brings out behaviours that we have to address and in some way learn to moderate. Leaders need to be careful not to crush the natural behaviour of boys while also helping them understand what behaviour is appropriate and where it is appropriate. Boys need strong leadership, time away from girls, good male role models, and many more things which we will consider later.

BOYS, SOCIETY AND CULTURE

There has been plenty of research into the changes in the perception of masculinity in our society, and some writing on the impact this may have on men in the church. In his books on the subject, *Hearing Men's Voices* and *Men and Masculinity*, Roy McCloughry examines what it means to be a man in today's world and explores the lives of 40 men, some of whom are genuinely asking whether men have any role left to play. The issues raised by McCloughry and others are numerous and, as they have a distinctive effect on men, they also influence boys and their perception of what it means to be a man. Where does all this leave a boy who is searching for a male role model?

- Women are free to live, develop careers and become leaders without needing men to be the traditional 'breadwinner' or to provide emotional and financial security.
- With the continued advances in embryonic research and the use of sperm banks, women no longer need a man in order to conceive.

- Many men are perceived by some women as having too much emotional baggage or being unreliable and feckless in their concern for others, including their families.

- Some men harm their own gender by holding to outdated, misogynistic attitudes to women, causing committed and capable women to see their futures without a male.

- There are plenty of examples of men who have failed their partners and their families, forcing women to cope alone because their male partner has moved on to another relationship or relationships.

- In some communities, particularly those where heavy industry, mining or other manual trades have diminished or vanished, men struggle to find their role. The women become the workers, with men searching or giving up on the search for employment, having no role and status in the community, suffering depression, and turning to drink or even drugs for survival or solace.

- Men are those who tend to leave the family home when a relationship breaks down, and men are far less likely than women to be single parents. When a man moves away from the family unit, he not only deprives his growing sons of a significant male role model in their lives, but also sends the message that it is men who give up, separate and go away.

- Men are more likely to do things in 'packs', whether going to the pub, to a rock concert or to a sporting event. This shows boys the importance of being in a group, but also demonstrates that men separate from their loved ones for these occasions.

- It is less common for men to be given or seen in 'caring' roles, such as childcare, primary age teaching and teaching assistant jobs. Men are therefore less likely to come into contact with boys, particularly at a younger age. In the UK, some statistics suggest that there is a slight increase in male teachers in schools serving pupils aged 3–11, but men still represent only around 15 per cent of the teaching population as a whole. If boys do not have a significant male role model, they may struggle to thrive, and those who have no male in their lives at home or at school until they reach secondary school age will not have seen what a 'man' can really be like.

According to writer and researcher Philip Zimbardo, in his book *Man (Dis)connected: How technology has sabotaged what it is to be male* (Rider, 2015), the development of boys into men is being negatively affected by modern technology. Zimbardo highlights a number of factors that have become much more prevalent through the use of the internet, including pornography, material greed, online gaming, seclusion, loneliness and inactivity. His argument is that boys are not learning to respect themselves or other people, are resentful of others who have more than they do, and are leading unhealthy lifestyles both physically and emotionally.

Following similar themes, the American doctor Leonard Sax, in his book *Boys Adrift* (Basic, 2009), also cites video games as a risk, along with poor education, overmedication of boys with behavioural issues and the lack of significant men in the lives of boys. When working with boys in the church for, say, three or four hours each week, we have to recognise the dangerous and damaging influences they face for the other 164 hours.

Men and Safeguarding

There is a significant paranoia expressed towards men who wish to, ask to or are gifted in working with children, and this is sometimes reflected in the recruitment of men to caring roles and the gender of volunteers who come forward to work with children in the church. There's still a lingering feeling in the church that children's work is feminine territory, and some men are actively discouraged from children's ministry. This feeling is based on the outdated theory that women have a nurturing ability that men don't, and that caring women are better for children than caring men. It ignores the fact that, as we have seen, boys need more than just mothering.

We are not helped by revelations about men in significant positions of authority, both within and outside the church, who have misused their power and authority to abuse boys. As a result, it is often considered dangerous to invite men to work with young people, and there can be a suspicion that the men who volunteer are doing so because of sexual attraction to children. It has been known for men involved in childcare or teaching very young people to be hounded out of their employment by paranoia, misinformation and rumour. While it is true that most people who sexually abuse children are men, and that churches have in the past been soft targets for child abusers, that obviously does not mean that all men in churches are potential child abusers! As we will keep seeing, men are essential in helping boys to reach their full potential as men, and unless churches take this seriously we will be responsible for a continued decline in the number of boys, male teenagers, and men in our worshipping communities.

Of course, men need to be appropriately checked through

the Disclosure and Barring Service (DBS) to ensure that they have no criminal convictions of violence against children and young people. Like all volunteers, men should be appropriately recruited with references and careful checking of lifestyle and temperament, according to the individual church's or denomination's Safer Recruitment policy. Like all volunteers, men should be supervised when working with children and young people, their behaviour should be monitored, and concerns should be addressed. But the church should be careful not to victimise male leaders or to shy away from actively recruiting men to work with boys and to be the vital role models that all boys need. We can't expect young Christian boys to grow into strong Christian men if they never see at close hand what a Christian man is.

CHAPTER 2

THE CHURCH AND BOYS

For boys, the church is not generally a place they want to be seen in. For boys growing up in a community with no church connections, the 'average' church is unlikely to attract them into friendship or faith. David Murrow's book *Why Men Hate Going to Church* (Nelson, 2005) raises a number of issues that we will look at later, and is based on the central claim that, rather than Christianity or any other faith, most men follow the religion of 'masculinity'.

BEHAVING

The way Christians should behave will be interpreted by everyone, including every Christian, differently, but churches have lost the drama, potential chaos, activity and movement that have been a feature of the church over the 2000 years of its development. No longer is worship particularly active or participatory, no longer do people wander in and out, and no longer is the church seen as the community meeting place and market place. Churches and church worship have become neat and tidy, ordered and regulated, and 'nice'.

We need to consider some of the implications of these issues.

DIFFERENT BEHAVIOUR

Boys who grow up in religious environments are expected to, and will often, behave differently from other boys of the same age. According to the 2002 report *Young Masculinities* by Stephen Frost, Ann Phoenix and Rob Pattman, young Muslim boys who don't talk dirty and do stick to their prayer routines are seen as both more mature and a little bit odd, as are Hindu boys who stick to their fasting and resist peer pressure. Their commitment to their faith marks them out as not being 'normal' but is also respected to an extent. Boys who are part of the church face huge challenges in school and in the community, and are open to bullying and abuse, just because they have the strength to be different.

BEHAVIOUR IN CHURCH

The church places expectations on the way boys should behave. Much of the worship in our churches is led from the front, with little visual stimuli and with congregational involvement only by invitation at certain set moments. As churches are run by adults and the majority of those attending are adults, the needs of the adults tend to dominate, at some cost to children and certainly to the detriment of boys.

I spoke recently to a mother of two lively boys aged seven and eight who had returned to church after quite a few years' absence. As it was a new and daunting experience for them, her boys were being a little noisy, asking questions about who the people were and what was happening, but they were not being overly disruptive. Sadly, after just a few minutes, a middle-aged woman behind them thought it was her duty to say to the mother, 'Please don't come back to church again until they [pointing to the boys] have learned to behave.' Understandably, the poor woman left in tears, with the boys trailing behind her, all three of them clearly getting the message that church was not for them.

Of course there should be due reverence for the worship space and for what God is doing as we worship, but we need to consider what is really happening in a situation like the one described above. Are the boys expressing their interest in and questions about what is happening? Are they bewildered by all the strange things that are happening around them? Are they being expected to behave in a way that is alien to their God-given nature?

WORSHIP AND READING

Worship in our churches still very often relies on a good level of literacy among the participants. As we have seen, many boys find reading somewhat challenging, yet in our churches there are things to be read from sheets of paper, from books handed to them, or from screens that may be obscured by pillars or by taller adults. Boys may disengage and behave in ways that adults don't find acceptable if there are too many words to be read.

MESS OR TIDINESS

Boys are generally untidy and cope with mess, noise and activity being all mixed up together. We see this when we look at the difference between most girls' and most boys' bedrooms. Boys' bedrooms are often dirty and untidy, with all sorts of unthinkable items hidden away and a particular distinctive smell. Boys' bedrooms represent the way most boys live and think, with mess being considered perfectly normal and acceptable.

In our churches we take planning and order very seriously.

We like everything to be neat and tidy, and we often don't like things to go wrong in any way. The church could gain from embracing some of the messiness that boys bring to our communities. We could see more creativity in our prayer, more spontaneity in our worship, and more variety in our activities, which would not only attract and keep boys and men but would also reach those on the fringe of church who feel they don't know what to do or when.

BEING GOOD, OR BEING A BOY

The church expects boys to be 'good', to be compliant and to be 'nice'. Our expectations about 'good' behaviour are full of personal subjective value judgements, often including the belief that boys will endure anything we throw at them and somehow be able to crush their naturally aggressive, active and lively attributes. However, many boys don't want to be seen as 'nice'. As we have already seen, boys want to be the centre of attention, they want to be winners, and they want to fight.

There is a very difficult balance to be struck here. On the one hand, we want boys to be boys and accept that they are made in the image of God, and, on the other, we want them to conform entirely to ways of behaving that are not masculine. The more we admonish boys for behaving like boys, the more we tell them, 'This is not a place for you.'

ROLE MODELS

Boys need to base their behaviour on credible male role models who either enhance the influence of the good dad at home or, where it is missing, replace that role. Yet many of the men in our churches are not the strong, credible men that boys need to look up to. David Murrow, in *Why Men Hate*

Going to Church, explores what the church does to aggressive and energetic men. He claims that, as a rule, it gives them administrative roles or asks them to take on far too much responsibility and wears them out. It piles on the pressure, which only adds to the burden of conformity that they may already face in the community and at work.

There are some men in churches who are strong leaders and attractive role models, whose masculinity has not been swallowed up by 'churchianity' and who show what God's plan for manhood is, but there are not enough of them. If boys in church are in need of good role models, it's no use giving them some of the odd characters we have in our churches, moulded by years of misunderstandings and false expectations of what it means to be a man. In churches, boys may struggle to see many men who they would like to be like. The male leaders are often a generation or two older than the boys themselves, more like grandfathers than role models. Boys are unwilling to stay in an institution or club where there are few people like them and even fewer who are the sort of person they would want to be.

THE FEMININE FACE OF THE CHURCH

Much of what a church looks and feels like, and what happens within it, is more attractive to girls than to boys. There is little wonder that the majority of boys, who may be less attracted to pastel colours, gentle artwork and flowers, are not entirely at home in the worship space. Those boys who struggle to connect and express their emotions are less likely to appreciate some of the sung worship that takes place. Boys, who like to be active rather than passive, may find many acts of worship dull and remote.

Let's consider some of the factors that make church less inviting for boys.

CHURCH LEADERSHIP

Many church leaders, now, are women, and that is a great thing. We can all benefit from women in leadership and the unique and special gifts that they bring, but this may come at a cost for boys if it means that they see no male leaders. Of course, some women in leadership are great leaders and some men in leadership are not great, but, if boys' experiences of leadership are all involving women, they are likely to assume that the church is principally for females.

CHURCH MEMBERSHIP AND ATTENDANCE

In most churches, boys are likely to see more girls and women than boys and men. There are plenty of stories of men who first started attending church as teenagers because the church was a good place to meet girls, but I wouldn't advocate that as a good evangelism strategy. It is not easy for boys to be in a place that doesn't represent them, where they are seen as the exception and not the rule. As we will see, boys need a 'peer group' in a way that most girls don't, so, if they find that they are frequently on their own as the only boy in church, they will not want to stay.

CHURCH APPEARANCE

Some very dedicated people work hard to make our churches clean and attractive places to be in, but they are not necessarily attractive to boys. Churches often have banners with gentle, pleasant pictures on them. There will almost always be flowers on display, and a great deal of work will have gone into their presentation. The church may have stained-glass windows telling stories or representing biblical characters, but often with pastel colours, feminine-looking angels and artistic representations that do not relate to the here-and-now. Boys are less likely to relate to or be able to appreciate the physical beauty of the building. Churches will be painted in neutral or pastel shades rather than the vivid primary colours that are more attractive to boys. The materials used at the front—be they robes worn by women and men or the altar frontal and other traditional materials— all appeal more to the feminine than the masculine. Of course, there are some boys who will not be put off by some of these things, but more girls are likely to enjoy them than boys.

There's not a great deal that can be done about these elements of the church's appearance, and it would be wrong to throw the baby out with the bathwater, bringing in wholesale change that would appeal to boys and men but would be very unhelpful for women and girls. But we need to try to view our worship space through the lens of boys, and accept that we will have to work harder to help them engage and feel at home.

WORSHIP CONTENT

As I commented earlier, worship in many churches is ill-suited to boys, as a great deal of it is word-based, with a clear reliance on literacy skills and a lack of opportunity to let off steam, make noise and run around. Boys, most of whom learn best in short bursts, with movement and participation, will not be learning much in many church services. Boys are also reluctant to sing, for reasons we will explore later.

DIFFICULT CONCEPTS

If boys and men are active, visionary and looking to succeed or be winners, there's a great deal about the way Christianity is delivered that will turn them off. Boys and men may struggle with some of our assumptions and concepts about faith and our expected spiritual responses. Teachings about concepts such as 'letting go' and 'submitting' can be culturally difficult for boys and are hard to think through from a practical and emotional point of view. It is much harder for boys to connect the 'teaching and learning' aspect of church with the internalised responses required. In general, women may be more accepting of the language and concepts involved.

THE CHILDREN'S WORK GENDER GAP

The church has a real problem with the reality that most adults who work with children are women. These workers are generally extremely dedicated, skilled, well-prepared and sacrificially dedicated to the ministry to which God has called them. They do all they can to nurture faith in young people and help their spirituality to develop. Boys are obviously not damaged by having women to enthuse them, but they will be greatly helped by seeing men working alongside those women.

CHURCH ATTENDANCE

Many mothers find it difficult if their partners do not share the Christian faith or their dedication to the life of the church. It is common for mums to struggle to church on a Sunday morning with children, while dads stay at home to have a rest, do some jobs or wash the car. Boys see this. They are being taken from home to be in a place they don't necessarily enjoy, while the main man in their life is at home doing other things. There will come a time for boys in this situation when they want to do what the men do—that is, not to go to church but to stay at home and do other stuff.

THE COMMUNITY FOR BOYS

The church community doesn't necessarily seem very inviting to many boys, despite our rhetoric and our promises to value and welcome everyone. Boys have particular needs, as outlined below. If those needs are not met, they will feel excluded from the 'club' that church can often resemble.

BOYS NEED COMMUNITY

For boys to grow well, they need a community of like-minded, similar boys around them. Peer group is really important for the social, spiritual and emotional development of boys. Boys who are unhelpfully influenced by the wrong peer group will suffer, but boys who have a positive peer group, based on the safety and security of a loving church family, will survive and thrive.

Boys in community are able to challenge each other, compare their problems, talk things through, fight and bond with each other. Boys who develop strong friendships also become very loyal to each other and to the group—so much so that if a church has a strong group of boys, the quality of the programme or activities doesn't matter too much, as they will attend out of their commitment to each other. Boys who do not have other boys with them in the church community will more than likely leave the church at some point, especially if (as we have just seen) their fathers are staying at home. The church will appear to be a place where people like them are not welcome, where they are exposed and unable to hide in the crowd, and where they are expected to conform to behaviour that is unnatural.

BOYS NEED TO BE PART OF A WIDER COMMUNITY

If a church is composed only of older people, there is something missing. If it is all women, there's something wrong. If a church community has no boys and few men, it is not what God intended it to be. Boys have a great deal to contribute to the life of any church. They bring passion, energy and even a challenge to leadership and 'old' ways of doing things. The church is a lesser place without them. Boys in church need to know, engage with and be engaged by the wider congregation. If boys do not feel they are welcome as part of the wider church group, they will not be inclined to attend, or will leave at the earliest point possible in their lives.

BOYS NEED A PLACE TO BE BOYS

After many years of training, writing and thinking through the issue, I am more and more convinced that there should be times when boys have activities that are just for boys. By the same token, I have no doubt that sessions just for girls do no harm either, but this highlights some concerns I have about the key uniformed organisations for young people in the UK. We know that boys do not attend Brownies or Guides; indeed, this is made a feature in some of the publicity material for the Guiding organisation, with quotes from young members saying things such as, 'I like it that there are no boys.' So we see that girls have a place to call their own, and activities that they can do without boys being present. The Girls' Brigade holds to similar rules, although some Girls'

Brigade groups have become Girls' Associations and joined with local Boys' Brigade companies.

Boys, on the other hand, now have no mainstream church-linked uniformed organisation that is just for them. Cubs and Scouts have, for some while, accepted girls as well as boys, and the Boys' Brigade can also choose to accept girls into its membership at all levels. I was hugely helped, challenged, encouraged and allowed to fail as well as succeed within a caring and supportive Boys' Brigade company, and I valued having time with other boys. I am not sure that the situation would have been the same had girls also been there. Many leaders of mixed uniformed groups tell me that, in their experience, girls are a moderating influence on the behaviour of the boys—and I think this could well be a problem! Boys do need time and space where they can be entirely themselves, along with their peers, without any pressures to conform.

BIBLICAL BALANCE

The Bible spans thousands of years of history, and much of it was written in times and cultures where men ruled the nations, the battles, the families and clans, and the temples. The Bible can therefore be difficult to read and interpret correctly for our more balanced and enlightened times. As we see the Christian faith that was once so popular with men now failing to attract them, we may need to consider what 'spin' our churches are putting on scripture. We will look later at how to use the Bible with boys, and characters from the Bible that they may relate to, but, for now, here are some issues to think through.

A MIRACULOUS GOD

The Bible is full of amazing, supernatural, incredible things that the Creator has done and continues to do. Churches pay lip service to these miraculous events, but, in our age of 'new enlightenment', we sometimes downplay them. We interpret them as being capable of scientific explanation, or simply put the biblical descriptions down to rather poetic language. Yet the miraculous, amazing and stunning will be attractive to boys if we fire up their imaginations and help them see that God is beyond their practical and scientific understanding.

THE FAITH OF THE FIGHT

Churches have moderated their language since the heady days of the 'fire and brimstone' preachers who condemned everyone in the congregation and the community alike. There is a risk, though, that we have made the Christian faith a bit too easy to get into, and the requirements for living a Christian life a little watered-down. Boys and men are yearning for a challenge and a fight: if Christianity is communicated as a 'soft option', there is nothing to motivate or challenge them in it. In Galatians 5:7, Hebrews 12:1 and 1 Corinthians 9:24, the writers speak of running a race, and that challenge needs to remain in our teaching.

THE NATURE OF GOD

We know that God is loving, gracious and forgiving, but we tend to minimise some of the Old Testament reflections of God's character. The Bible is full of battles, destruction and struggle, as well as some of the more palatable concepts. The Old Testament people of God, like us, were on a journey of failure and destruction, forgiveness and rehabilitation. The church can be in danger of getting the focus and balance wrong, with an overemphasis on love, grace and being 'nice', at the cost of the true complete picture.

THE NATURE OF JESUS

As well as the visual images of Jesus to be seen in children's Bibles and picture books, which portray a gentle, kind-looking man, often with pure white robe and long flowing hair, we are inclined to give Jesus attributes that he probably didn't have, ignoring some of the challenges that he went through. If the incarnation means that Jesus was fully human as well as fully divine, some of the songs we sing, particularly at Christmas, are pushing a myth that misrepresents the truth and is a turn-off for boys. Was Jesus gentle, meek, mild, uncrying, sweetly sleeping, kind, obedient, our childhood pattern, and so on? Of course, Jesus was an entirely unique baby and child, but this portrayal does nothing to help boys who are looking for a hero they can relate to. The tough battles Jesus fought, the things he said that were challenging and less popular as texts to preach from, and the way he faced hatred, persecution and death all have a part to play in a church that is seeking to attract men and boys.

CHAPTER 3

WORKING WITH BOYS

In later chapters, we will look at some specific details of what to do with boys in worship, prayer, and so on. Underlying all we do, though, are some basic ideas that will make working with boys a little easier.

BOYS AT AN EARLY AGE

If we are to help the boys in our churches grow successfully into Christian men, we need to include them in the activities of the church from the earliest point on.

You will have heard what the Jesuits say: 'Give me the boy until he is seven, and I will give you the man.' We know that boys develop rapidly and begin to change, aged 4–5, when testosterone becomes particularly evident in them, so we also know that they are beginning to be formed into men even at that young age. Psychologist Sami Timimi wrote a book called *Naughty Boys* (Palgrave Macmillan, 2005), exploring the influences on boys. He identified that Western society encourages children to engage in antisocial behaviour, and that the influences become embedded early on.

Here are some things we can do to promote the inclusion of boys more successfully.

• Talk about the importance of work with young children. Some churches may consider work in the crèche or preschool to be simply child-minding, of no spiritual or social consequence. Yet we know that, as young minds are being formed, they are open to the influences of their environment. Therefore, through the use of simple repeated Bible stories, songs with some spiritual input and a caring Christian environment, young children will pick up the atmosphere and will become changed by it.

- Encourage men to work with young children. As we know, this is a difficult issue. Many men do not think that work with babies and toddlers has anything to do with them, and some parents may not be willing to see men working with their young children. Yet little boys need to have men around them in all areas of their lives in order to understand that what they do is normal, not only for children but for men too.

- Remember that boys are different. In a room full of toddlers, it is easy to see them all as a 'group' and not as lots of individuals. If we keep in the back of our minds that boys are indeed different from girls, we will naturally provide a varied programme that will appeal to the boys' sense of energy and activity, and we will also recognise and understand some of their more aggressive and antisocial behaviour.

PROGRAMME PLANNING FOR BOYS

Whatever resources we have available in our churches, there are some basic principles that need to be followed when we use our material to plan a programme for the session.

Remember that boys need opportunities to be physically

active and to 'let off steam', particularly if they are coming to the session straight from having to be quiet and conform in the main church service. This active time need only be short and focused, although in some church environments it may not be practical, due to space and noise restrictions. If possible, it can be helpful to give boys the opportunity to go outside and get some fresh air for a few minutes. Before church, see if the boys, and any girls who choose to, could meet for a few minutes and play some active games before calming down for the beginning of the service.

Many children's workers like to think that they are good at telling stories, and will ramble on for rather too long. This is fine for a few boys who may be good auditory learners, but, for those who need activity and action in order to learn, it will lead to boredom and disconnection. Each section of the programme needs to be short enough to offer variety while also providing some depth. Avoid doing anything that lasts longer than ten minutes, and, within that time period, offer occasional opportunities to pause, breathe in deeply and stretch.

We do not want to undermine the valid and valuable teaching that God made us all and loves us all, but we also want to recognise those boys who have particular skills and talents. In some communities, the very thought of saying to a child that they are a winner is offensive, as it means that other children are by definition losers. In our work with boys, we need to be careful not to reinforce negative self-image or make the sessions testosterone-filled challenges, but there is a place for a bit of competition and recognition of success in races, games, quizzes, and so on. Boys enjoy being winners.

Check your programme to make sure there is a variety of

activities that will engage both boys and girls. These activities could include games, role play, drama, craft, singing, movement, active prayers and team or pairs work, as well as other elements.

Plan some sessions where you throw out all the plans and do something entirely different—remembering that boys with particular needs, particularly Asperger's syndrome and autism, will appreciate having a bit of warning that this is going to happen. You could bring in a speaker or a drama group, do some graffiti (where allowed), go for a walk, visit the children's work in another local church, play some games on some open land or the local park, do a whole session singing worship songs, or just play lots of games. This will help the boys who like variety and a mix of inputs, and will give everyone a different experience.

MATERIALS THAT WORK WITH BOYS

If you are looking for really successful material for boys, you will be aware of a problem with the materials that are currently published for use with children in church settings. This problem is a bit of a vicious circle. The majority of the children in our churches and church groups are girls. Publishers tend to produce materials that best suit the majority market, in order to keep the product selling and therefore viable—so boys are not encouraged to join or stay in our churches and church groups.

Some church children's groups meet in rooms, halls, kitchens, lobbies, vestries, bell towers or cupboards (yes, I have seen them all!) that provide little room for moving around, and where the 'main' church can easily hear what is going on and be disturbed by it. Users of the published materials can be fairly hard to please, and will make it clear in feedback if there are too many physical or noisy activities to suit their groups and the physical environments in which they work.

Most adult volunteers (perhaps up to 90 per cent) who work with children are women, and they are the 'gatekeepers' for the type of materials purchased. They are likely to be attracted to materials designed in a way that appeals to them, and are also likely to want materials including activities that are more girl-friendly and less boisterous.

Much of the material, even in children's Bibles, avoids the more challenging, bloody or unpleasant parts of scripture, focusing instead on the 'nice', palatable sections. For instance, the story of Noah's ark is often used because it provides the opportunity for great artwork. Rarely, if ever, do we find materials that take the story further, where Noah disobeys God, gets drunk, and so on.

The design of Christian literature for children is more attractive to girls than to boys. Most girls like to see pastel colours and rounded shapes, whereas most boys would rather have primary colours and angular design. Publishers of secular comics and magazines for children have huge research budgets and are able to make products that hit the target market perfectly. Those publications clearly prove the point about design.

All of these factors mean that children's group resources tend to be less suitable for boys. This is a real challenge for hard-pressed, very busy but also very dedicated volunteers who feel called to work with our children. They need to use materials in which ideas are provided for them and some of the preparation is already done.

In order to rebalance the materials we use and the activities we do with our groups, we need to follow a few simple steps, seeking out resources that will work better for boys.

- Boys generally prefer to follow stories through comic versions with little text to read, where the vivid pictures give visual clues to what the words are communicating. There are now some excellent visual Bibles, comics that tell the Christmas and Easter stories, and similar products that should be introduced in order to help boys engage with scripture.

- Boys enjoy challenge and competition, and those who are into video games and quests will be attracted to materials such as the *Guardians of Ancora* game. *Guardians of Ancora* has been developed by Scripture Union in England and Wales to provide a positive, challenging game based on biblical stories. Boys can join in, become a character, fight and overcome challenges and move up levels in very much the same way as they would in the less wholesome or helpful secular equivalents. *Guardians of Ancora* describes itself on its website (http://guardiansofancora.com) as 'a world-class tablet game for 8- to 11-year-olds offering an amazing virtual world and an immersive interactive experience of Bible stories', and is simply great for boys.

Look at all the materials and resources your church has available for boys, and spend some time comparing them with equivalent secular resources and materials. Then consider how you can make small changes, introducing a little more activity or better visuals, to bring them closer to the needs of boys.

Ask the children what they think of the booklets, pictures

and other materials you use. Invite them to talk freely about what they most enjoy and what they enjoy less. Children are likely to give you the answers they think you are seeking, so be careful not to lead them in the way you want their responses to go. Don't be afraid to 'go with the flow'. Boys can make suggestions that you are not expecting or ask questions that take the whole session in different directions. Girls, of course, may do the same, but are more inclined to go along with whatever the leader is suggesting or doing.

Plan your programme with a focus on both practical and active elements, as well as spiritual content. Some groups can be dominated by work to be done on 'art activities'. Sticking and colouring, with lots of glitter, is likely to bore boys more quickly than it bores girls.

Think about how your materials communicate Jesus. If the programme tends to focus more on the lovely things Jesus said and did, and less on the reality of the fight, his walk to death and his fully human experience of pain, boys will be less attracted to their Saviour.

BOYS NEED BOUNDARIES

Boys are likely to push the boundaries of your patience and planning. They will fidget, fight, make stupid noises at the wrong times, behave badly, and generally test their leaders to the limits. Of course, those who volunteer to work with children in a church setting do not want to spend all their time trying to keep order or implementing rules, and the children who come do not want to attend an over-regimented session. On the other hand, less secure children and those who prefer some sense of order, particularly girls, will feel disturbed if boundaries are not implemented. Ultimately, the gospel message deserves to be listened to, as do those who are called to communicate it.

The following suggestions are likely to work equally well with boys as with girls, and will help the group to settle into learning together.

As boys are less able to see and interpret non-verbal signs of communication, such as a stare, a glance or a frown, it is necessary to make clear when you are not satisfied with the behaviour that is going on around you. This will need to be communicated both by your expressions and by what you say. Develop an action or activity that is clear and reminds all the children, including the boys, that it is time to pay attention, to stop or to listen. Avoid using a whistle: children are far more valuable than sheep or sheepdogs! Here are a few possibilities:

- Hold your hands high in the air and clap twice, expecting the group to mirror your action.

- Use a short burst of a familiar piece of music, worship song or pop song to attract the attention of the children.

- Count down from five, and wait at the end until all of the children have stopped and looked in your direction.

- Develop a chant based on the name of the group. Get the children to help you do this, as that will encourage a level of commitment to taking part and doing what is expected. The chant can be shouted, said, whispered, and so on, so that the children get used to being loud and being quiet together.

- Use a percussion instrument to tap out a short rhythm, with the children being expected to reply with the same rhythm. This can be repeated until all of the children have stopped what they are doing and are looking to you for guidance.

Create a set of rules that should be followed by all members of the group. Explore with them what behaviour, language and attitudes they consider to be acceptable and unacceptable behaviour. Then work on a set of ground rules that are displayed and referred to regularly. The 'rules' or 'guidelines' should focus on the positive rather than the negative. Try to keep the number to a maximum of around five, so that they can easily be remembered. Here are some examples that you may wish to use:

- We will always listen to the leaders and each other when we are talking and praying.

- We will keep everyone else safe by not hurting them or causing harm.

- We will help each other to have fun, and not stop others from enjoying themselves.

- We will look after all the good things we have, including each other.

- We will learn something new by taking part and helping others to take part.

- We will be lively, creative, and quiet at the right times.

The children's 'ownership' of these guidelines will be very important, as group members who have contributed to their development are much more likely to follow them. It also follows that the group will, in their own ways, show their frustration or disappointment to those children who don't conform.

Make sure that the boys in particular are reminded of the consequences of poor behaviour. This means that there needs to be a set procedure for those children who do not behave appropriately, and some level of agreement and parity in the way things are dealt with by the leaders. Children are very adept at spotting the cracks in any rules, and will easily work out and exploit the situation if a leader is considered to be 'soft' and easy to mess around. Despite the way we might see it, boys do not thrive in an anarchic setting where there are no rules and no boundaries. They thrive when they can explore and express themselves within defined boundaries.

Nip difficult situations in the bud by spotting boys who will trigger poor behaviour in others, or keeping apart those who find it hard not to fight each other. Simply by having leaders sitting with the children and interacting with them, many behavioural problems can be prevented. To have a leader sitting between two boys who wind each other up diffuses the situation.

Remember that children will forget rules over a long period of time, so it's worth revisiting them occasionally and doing some additional work on them to check that they are still relevant and meet the changing needs of the group. This is a particularly helpful thing to do at the start of a new year when you may have some new children joining the group.

Never speak or shout over the children. Make it clear, by waiting, that you want them to hear and respond to what you are saying. Once you have done the chant, hand-clap, or whatever else is done to draw attention, simply wait patiently for the children to stop what they are doing, to look, and to listen. Then talk calmly while lowering your voice and glancing around to make sure that all the children are listening hard. This may take a little while for the children to get used to, and leaders may be tempted to jump in and start talking even if there are a few children who have not yet stopped. Stick at it, because, once it has become a habit, it makes the whole group work better together.

Speaking or shouting over children has three negative consequences. First, the children know that they can carry on doing what they choose to do, without regard for you or for the other children in the group. Second, it represents a loss of the authority and respect that you are encouraging the children to have for you. Third, the general volume and noise made by the boys in particular will increase as your volume increases, resulting in too much noise, complaints from the 'adult' congregation next door, and headaches all round.

If you have consistent behavioural challenges with a number of boys, you need to go through a process to discover what the issues may be. First, find out whether the boys who are struggling to behave have got other significant issues in their lives that may be affecting their behaviour. Second, take a careful and critical look at the programme you are delivering, considering whether there is enough variety, activity and creativity to keep the boys engaged. Try to reflect on the points in the session that went well for the group and for those boys, and the times when things went awry. Work out whether you can avoid those times or do things differently in order to keep the boys more engaged. Third, start to work through your behaviour sanctions, which may include involving parents. Do not be afraid to ask a child not to attend if all else has failed and the disruption being caused is proving damaging to the other children and to the leaders.

Boys need adult interaction

There are some things that most boys enjoy and most girls don't. Boys enjoy really poor jokes, horror stories and useless facts and figures. They like to discuss football and the latest heroes of the game. As they move into adolescence, boys may want to talk through issues about the obvious vocal and physical changes they are going through, and their attitudes to girls may be changing. It is really important that, from time to time, leaders make space in the programme for boys to talk these things through with each other and with leaders, and to listen to what others have to say.

Boys have things they can teach us! Group leaders should show an interest in the things that the boys are into outside church, whether it's video games, the latest card collection craze, sports, model making, fishing, or whatever. If a leader is willing to listen and learn, it shows boys that we are all learning together. It helps with the trust and bonding process between boy and man, and will make them much more likely to listen to what we have to say when we talk about our faith and what we believe.

Allow boys to open up about the issues that they face in their lives. This is not easy to do, and will not be easy for the boys in the group until they are sure they have a supportive peer group around them and leaders who genuinely want to know and want to help. Boys may need reminding that there is a great deal of strength in knowing yourself well enough to recognise that you have issues, and being willing to admit it and get some guidance. Leaders can help with this by sharing a little of what happened to them as children (as long as this doesn't become an ageist rant, along the lines of 'When I was your age... You lot don't know you're born!') Boys will appreciate men who are willing to share their challenges and be open about what they have faced in the past.

Be aware that boys will not always be willing to raise the subjects that are on their mind, so some help from leaders may be needed. Talk with boys as appropriate about the cultural pressures in the world and society that they face, including materialism, the pressure to succeed, financial pressures, bereavement, pornography, sexuality and relationships. This can be done by looking at the headlines in the paper or on the news, or simply raising a subject and seeing where it goes. Try to help boys to understand their world from a biblical point of view, and give them the skills to look to the Bible to seek answers and support.

SPECIAL NEEDS AND BOYS

One of the most exciting and intriguing things about God's creative power is that he made us all different, with our individual needs. However, there are some diagnosed 'special needs' that have a significant effect on the way some boys behave, respond socially and take in information, which we need to consider briefly.

We may have our own views on some of these issues. We may think that some unwelcome behaviour is because of 'bad parenting' or some other social reason. Whatever our personal views, we need to take what we are told seriously, and do all we can, as servants of God, to help the boys in our care.

More boys have some of the more common and obvious special needs than girls. It is thought that up to five times more boys than girls are diagnosed as being somewhere on the autism spectrum. One form of autism is Asperger's syndrome, which was defined in the 1940s and, at the time, was assumed not to affect girls at all. Since then, research has found that girls are likely to be better at covering up the signs of the syndrome, and so may be up to half as likely to have it as boys.

With ADD or ADHD (Attention Deficit or Attention Deficit Hyperactivity Disorder), four times as many boys are diagnosed than girls, although some research suggests that this is because the symptoms in girls are less obvious than those in boys. With dyslexia, again it is thought that more boys than girls have the condition, which can cause problems with reading and numeracy, but some experts question the proportion of boys who have the condition.

Each of these particular needs stems from different issues with the brain, and they all need to be taken into account when we are working with boys. Here are some points that may be helpful.

First, research the theory. If you are working with a boy who has one of these diagnosed conditions, find out as much as you can about it in general, and how it affects him and his behaviour in particular. Read up on the syndrome, and reflect on your experiences of the boy concerned to see if his behaviour matches that described. There is a huge number of websites that give information and support, and the booklet *Top Tips on Welcoming Special Children* (from Scripture Union) is a handy, short guide with some useful suggestions.

Find out as much as possible about the individual boy concerned, from his parent or carer. Many parents will not want to have this conversation, as they may fear that the children's group or leader could refuse to work with their child. Explain to parents that you want to do the very best you can for their son, but, in order to do that, you need to know how his syndrome affects him at home and at school, what level of support he receives at school, whether he is on medication and how it affects him, and so on. If possible, and with the parent's consent and support, try to talk to the boy's teacher or teaching assistant at school to get a clearer idea of how best to support the boy, and what may trigger his fear, anger or frustration.

Where possible, try to provide a level of specific support for the boy, particularly in the areas where he may be less comfortable or confident. A boy with dyspraxia, which can affect coordination, may need a bit of extra help and encouragement when playing physical games. A boy with dyslexia may need a little help with reading the text on the activity sheet. A boy with a degree of Asperger's may struggle with some of the social activities that take place, and could want to avoid eye contact. The more you know of the boy and the support he gets elsewhere, the better you can handle him and treat him as the equal in God's eyes that he is. There is a strong argument for making sure that boys are getting this support from a man, as this again breaks down barriers and forms a helpful and aspirational bond.

Encourage other children to take some responsibility. Boys can be cruel to each other, and many boys who have autism testify to being bullied at school. Some of that bullying may come from a fear of difference. It may therefore be appropriate, with subtlety and confidentiality, to share with some of the boys that others may not find all activities as easy as they do. Boys who form a bond can also be extremely supportive and kind to each other, and some boys will respond to being asked to support one with particular needs. In a church environment, you will aim to have groups in which everyone is accepting and tolerant of each other, and where care comes not only from the leaders but also from the children themselves.

Offer support, and encourage other children to help, with care and sensitivity. Those boys who have particular needs do not need it to be highlighted and made obvious. Some boys with autism are encouraged to make that clear to other children and adults at first meeting, so that others have some understanding of why they behave as they do—but that is not generally the case.

Share your plans with the boys. Many boys with particular needs, and others too, will be helped by having a good idea of what the programme for the session or club is going to be. As we know, boys thrive within boundaries, and, if they know roughly what is going to happen, they can prepare themselves for the noise, activity or interaction that they find most difficult.

For boys who are autistic and therefore need order and structure in order to thrive, the way you use the room, hall or space that you have is really important. If you can, and without making a big thing of it, try to ensure that the different activities take place in different areas. For instance, boys will then know that the prayer time will be near the door, or the worship will be by the table, and so on. Again, this helps them prepare for what to expect. Some boys will not be comfortable in the middle of a room with no walls close by, so you may want to consider ensuring that those that seek the security of a barrier next to them can sit by the wall.

You can learn from children with special needs. Boys who have some level of autism are very often extremely intelligent and may have particular passions and interests, about which they are very knowledgeable. Not only will such boys be able to explain their particular need and how it can affect them, but they should also be given every opportunity to share their interest enthusiastically with leaders.

Some boys will have difficulty in being told what to do, particularly if they have thought of a different way to reach the same or a better result. It is not a sign of weakness to offer boys with particular needs an appropriate level of choice in how to do an activity, or in what to do. For instance, boys who struggle in a social environment will not want to play games that involve too much physical contact, and to force them to join in may cause a degree of distress and disruption, as well as emotional harm.

We know that many boys will fidget and move around, fiddle with things and generally struggle to sit still, but those boys who have a diagnosed issue that affects their ability to concentrate and pay attention will need help in managing their fidgeting. This may involve giving some boys a stress-busting piece of foam, a lump of sticky tack, a pipe cleaner or a small piece of material to play with while they are listening. Their movement as they fiddle with the item will help them to listen and concentrate.

Boys who struggle to conform or behave well, because of their special needs, can often be managed by offering them aspiration and praise. Many boys will respond well to being given a role of some responsibility, and will concentrate very hard on fulfilling that role. To give them opportunities also gives them some self-esteem, and reinforces the value that God sees in each one of us, no matter what we are like.

For many of us, eye contact is the main method we use both to communicate our message and to interpret whether our listeners have heard and understood what we are saying. However, many boys with autism will feel intimidated by eye contact, and will involuntarily look slightly down and to the side if they feel vulnerable in this way. Therefore, while eye contact will work for the majority, don't expect it from everyone, and don't interpret lack of eye contact as lack of interest or as a challenge to your authority.

Boys and learning styles

Many of the suggestions later in this book are based on these three principles of communicating with and learning with children, particularly boys. Put simply, boys will not learn well if they are placed in a dull, sterile environment, have nothing to listen to, do, or see, and have to be still.

An understanding of different learning styles will help those educating children and young people to discover how to impart and share knowledge to meet the needs of the individual learner. In Canada, Dave Csinos has done some research and development in what he calls 'spiritual styles', which is being followed through in the UK by means of 'Roots' teaching materials. Boys will have particular preferences in the way they learn best, so it is important to make sure that all teaching is delivered in a range of ways.

One of the simplest learning style theories came out of the United States and its accelerated learning programmes, and is known simply as VAK. (A great deal of information about VAK and other learning styles theories is available in books and on the internet.) The VAK learning style theory talks of three main preferences for learning: visual, auditory and kinaesthetic (or movement). The theory suggests that all learners, however young or old, have a dominant style. As learners, boys (and girls) will use all three styles to receive, interpret and learn new information, but, according

54

to the VAK theory, one or two of these receiving styles is normally dominant. Learners will usually use the style that is most dominant, but they may revert to a different style for different tasks.

Some theorists suggest that our learning style changes as the way we are taught changes, but this may have a negative effect on how much we learn. For instance, once we are in an academic environment, we are more likely to be taught in an auditory way, which may not be best for us.

Whatever the learning style of each individual boy in our groups, we need to deliver information in all three styles so that all the boys can learn well.

- **Visual:** Visual learners enjoy looking, and they are able to remember what they see really well. Some of them are good at writing and reading, while others will struggle with those skills. To communicate well visually, you will need to use movement, colour, visual aids, pictures, DVDs, films, costumes and artefacts. When communicating with visual learners, we may need to reinforce spoken information a number of times to help boys connect the images they are looking at with the words we are saying.

- **Auditory:** Auditory learners enjoy listening and following instructions. They may speak to themselves or form silent words on their lips. They gain more from explanation than from diagrams. To help them learn, we need to tell stories and give clear explanations, describe things that stretch their imaginations, and do group activities that involve sharing ideas and listening to each other.

- **Kinaesthetic:** Kinaesthetic learners learn best when they are able to move around, use up some energy and touch items. They will lose concentration when listening unless they can take notes or have something to do with their hands. We can meet their needs best by breaking up our sessions into small chunks, with some movement and activity. Boys will appreciate having something to fiddle with in their hands, and gentle background music may keep them more on-task.

This learning style theory is just that—a theory that may work with some boys and may not with others. Because of the differences between the brains of boys and girls, boys are more inclined to need movement when learning, and are less able to switch quickly between different talks and inputs. This suggests that the 'myth' that men can't multitask may have some truth in it. The key is to provide variety of style and input, meeting the varied needs of boys in our groups.

Boys and Christian belief

Boys find it a challenge to express what they believe and to fully understand the nature of Christian belief. Again, this is related to the way their brains are wired, with fewer connections between the emotional and the physical. The dynamic, 'muscular' aspects of Christian faith are not always communicated to them, and issues about submission and 'giving in' can cause boys some confusion and doubt. We need to do all we can to help boys grow in their faith and to know what their faith is all about.

To help boys think through the reasons for their own Christian beliefs, we need to go through the basics with them in creative and interesting ways. The suggested programme of teaching on the following pages is based on the Apostles'

Creed. When discussing faith issues with boys, ensure that you keep to some basic parameters:

- **Let boys share with you:** The church has learned a lot about faith development over the past 30 or 40 years, and most children's workers are now aware that children have an inborn spirituality, which we need to encourage and nurture. In the past, it was believed that children were empty vessels and that only when we filled them with knowledge would they find faith for themselves. Boys may not be aware of their own spirituality as children, but God is with them just as much as he is with adults.

- **Allow questions:** As boys grow, they will also have more questions, some of which may be challenging to our own faith and understanding. In those circumstances, we may feel ourselves becoming defensive and trying to give closed and easy answers. However, we must encourage this questioning of our faith, as it shows a deeper seeking in the lives of the boys who ask, and also strengthens us as we seek out the answers for ourselves.

- **Don't have all the answers:** However good a theologian we may be, none of us fully understands God or his plans for us and the world, so none of us has all the answers. As boys struggle with their own insecurities and doubts, it is a great help to them to meet leaders, particularly men, who likewise don't know all the answers. In reality, there will be some questions that we simply can't answer, and others that we will need to think about and research.

- **Don't create false heroes:** In some homes and schools, brothers are compared with each other, with the oldest perhaps held up as the standard for the others to reach. Likewise, some churches include people who have grown up in the church and gone on to do great things in church ministry and service, who then become mythologised as perfect examples of Christian virtue. If we are frequently challenging the boys we work with to be like these boys of the past, we may be setting up an ideal that they realise they can never attain.

- **Challenge:** It's helpful to have occasional debates or discussions that tackle the heart of Christian belief, with a leader or carefully chosen visitor playing 'devil's advocate' to challenge and question the boys on their depth and understanding of faith. This will highlight which boys are exploring the issues, which are struggling to understand the gospel message, and which seem to have a balanced personal faith.

- **Question time:** Again, you can sometimes bring in men from your church or other churches to face a barrage of questions from the boys, and to open up conversation and discussion. Encourage the boys to prepare questions in advance and not to shy away from difficult ones.

- **Question box:** Make available a box, some paper and some pens so that boys can submit their own questions about faith, prayer and Christian lifestyle. Some boys will find it easier to submit questions in this way rather than speaking them out loud.

EXPLORING CHRISTIANITY: THE APOSTLES' CREED
In the following seven-part exploration of the Christian faith, basic questions are suggested for each section or phrase of

the Apostles' Creed, to help open up discussion. There is also an activity suggestion and a Bible reference where relevant. This exercise could be done as a series of short sessions over several weeks, or you could complete it in one go, perhaps on a day away. You may well want to look at the questions yourself in advance, or work through the sessions with your church leader or someone else with some additional biblical knowledge. The questions are open-ended and should enable a little discussion and a range of views to be aired.

BACKGROUND TO THE APOSTLES' CREED

This creed is a statement of faith that is shared by many Christian denominations across the world and is recited regularly in worship in churches that use liturgy. It is thought to have been developed in around AD390 by St Ambrose, who was a bishop in Milan. However, similar statements of faith were already circulating, and the Apostles' Creed as it is known today probably took shape over a number of years.

PART 1

I believe in God, the Father almighty,
creator of heaven and earth.

Read these phrases out together at least twice, and refer to the creation narrative to be found in Genesis 1. Then explore the following questions:

- If God created everything, who created God?
- What does it mean to 'create'?
- Do we think that God's creation took place over seven days, as we now understand 'days' to be?
- What is heaven like?

Spend some time in pairs, talking about creation and then drawing the best thing you can think of about God's creation.

PART 2

I believe in Jesus Christ, God's only Son, our Lord,
who was conceived by the Holy Spirit,
born of the Virgin Mary...

Read out these phrases together, a few times, in rhythm to a basic clapping beat. Remind the group of the Christmas story of Mary being greeted by an angel, and her commitment to have the child even though she was still a virgin. Some care may need to be taken in this explanation, depending on the age, understanding and maturity of the boys in the group. Then explore these questions:

• How could God have a son?

• Why did he send his son to be with the people on earth?

• Who is the Holy Spirit, and what does the Holy Spirit do?

• How would you describe Mary?

Spend a little time in silence, imagining Mary's feelings when the angel came to tell her that she would be giving birth to God's only son.

PART 3

Jesus suffered under Pontius Pilate,
was crucified, died, and was buried;
he descended into hell.

Read these phrases out a few words at a time, with the boys repeating each phrase after you. Then invite one or two boys to take the 'leader' role and read them again. Next, explore the following questions, with special reference to the role of Pilate and the crucifixion from Matthew 27:11–66.

- How did Jesus suffer after he was arrested?
- Why didn't he simply give up, deny being God's son, and decide not to go through with the crucifixion?
- Why was Jesus crucified like a common thief?
- What does the creed mean when it says that he went to hell?

Ask the boys to imagine they are watching Jesus being crucified. What would it look like? What would the noises around be like? Who else would be there?

PART 4

On the third day he rose again;
he ascended into heaven;
he is seated at the right hand of the Father,
and he will come to judge the living and the dead.

Read the passage out together, first very quietly and then loudly, as if celebrating. Then consider the following questions, referring to the Easter narratives in John 20 and Luke 24.

- Was Jesus really fully dead? If he was, what power made him rise again?
- If you had been one of the disciples, would you have believed he was alive if you had seen him?

- What does it mean to 'ascend'?

- Why has Jesus returned to heaven?

Think a little more about heaven. Sit in a circle and ask each boy to say one word that they think might describe heaven.

PART 5

I believe in the Holy Spirit,
the holy catholic and apostolic Church,
the communion of saints…

Say these lines one at a time, with the boys repeating each of them. Then explain that this section has three different ideas in it. First, it mentions the Holy Spirit, the third part of the Trinity of God alongside the Father and the Son. Then we think about the importance of the Christian Church across the world, and then we remember the followers of Christ throughout the last 2000 years. Discuss the following questions:

- Does the Holy Spirit work today?

- Why is the church important?

- What should churches and Christians do?

- Who are the 'saints'?

Open up a short time of discussion about who the 'saints' are by talking through some of the key figures in your spiritual development. Really, to be a saint means to be a follower of Jesus and to serve other people. Who are the saints in the lives of the boys?

PART 6

(I believe in) the forgiveness of sins,
the resurrection of the body,
and the life everlasting. Amen

Split the group into three, and allocate one of the phrases to each smaller group. Ask them to say their phrase when you point to them. Again, there are three different ideas here, including what it may mean to experience 'the resurrection of the body'. In essence, this means that, at the end of time, we will all be renewed. Revelation 21 could help a little with this idea, but it is not an easy concept for children or adults to grasp. Open up discussion based on these questions:

- Why does God continue to forgive people?

- How easy is it to forgive someone fully?

- If you got a new body, what would it be like?

- Would everlasting life be like this life?

Ask the boys to be quiet and think about the key three things they want to do or achieve in their life on earth. They can write the three things down on a small piece of paper and take it home to keep safely.

PART 7

I believe in God, the Father almighty,
creator of heaven and earth.

I believe in Jesus Christ, God's only Son, our Lord,
who was conceived by the Holy Spirit,
born of the Virgin Mary,

suffered under Pontius Pilate,
was crucified, died, and was buried;
he descended into hell.
On the third day he rose again;
he ascended into heaven,
he is seated at the right hand of the Father,
and he will come to judge the living and the dead.

I believe in the Holy Spirit,
the holy catholic and apostolic Church,
the communion of saints,
the forgiveness of sins,
the resurrection of the body,
and the life everlasting. Amen

Give each boy a copy of the Apostles' Creed and encourage everyone to say it out loud slowly, remembering that some boys will not find it easy to read and say.

Ask them to decide, in small groups or pairs, on the bits of the creed that they still find difficult to understand. Then have some open discussion to consider those parts and to try to take their understanding a little further.

Ask the boys, in the same small groups, to work on a rewrite of the creed in language and a style that may make it easier to say and understand. Then try to bring some of those fresh ideas and concepts together, to make a final product that may be a mixture of ideas from each smaller group. If possible, get the final version printed off and give it to the boys. It could also be used in church worship as a recognition of the work they have done and their increased learning and understanding.

A FAITH OF THEIR OWN

Children and adults come to faith and are aware of God working in their lives in a range of ways. Some will say that there was never really a time when they were not aware of God in their lives, and that as they grew, so their faith grew too. Other people may be able to talk about a particular occasion or even a number of occasions when they made definite commitments and recommitments to following Jesus. Yet others in our churches may not be able to talk about their own personal faith at all. Children are aware of the people in many churches who attend out of a sense of duty, because of social expectations, or simply because they have always done so, and may never have come to a living faith in Jesus themselves. Boys who have had the advantage of growing up in the church and are from a 'Christian' home, or those who have been carefully nurtured by good-quality and dedicated children's workers, may have learned to live their faith through their parents and leaders. At some point, these boys may need a personal challenge to step forward in faith for themselves.

There is a great deal of faith development research and theory by James Fowler and others, and the book by Francis Bridger, *Children Finding Faith* (SU, 2000), is a good introduction to some of these issues. Boys will not grow into believing, active, strong Christian men if they do not know what it is to have a faith of their own rather than simply going through the motions. We can help them to do this in a variety of ways.

Introduce the boys to a range of Christian men from within the church and from other churches. Ask those men to talk with the boys about their journey of faith, mentioning any particular moments of decision and commitment. It will also be helpful if those men can share and answer questions about the challenges that the Christian life can bring.

Leaders' testimonies are also important. If boys are to relate to their leaders and model their spiritual lives and development on the significant adults around them, they need to know their leaders' stories of faith. In my experience, many people who are called to ministry with children are surprisingly reluctant to share their Christian journey. This doesn't help those children to learn what the Christian journey is about.

It is vital to incorporate into your teaching plans and programmes carefully handled opportunities for boys to respond, through prayer and activity, to what God may be saying to them. The old-style 'altar call' during children's and youth events has generally been discontinued. Such calls were often accompanied by a degree of emotional force and pressure, which has been described as spiritual abuse. However, it also means that we are lacking explicit opportunities to invite boys to respond to what God is saying through the Holy Spirit to them. Leaders who have a good and growing relationship with the boys in the group should not shy away from an occasional opportunity to mention God's plan for each boy present, along with God's call for them to respond to him.

More will be said about 'male Christianity' later in this book, when we consider how to communicate the Christian faith through the Bible, but for now we need to remember that Christ was fully human and fully male, so the Christian faith is, in some sense, a masculine set of beliefs. Boys need to know that being a Christian is a hard rather than a soft option. To be a developing Christian may mean having to stand up for what is right despite peer pressure to do the opposite, to fight the negative influences found in our world, and to live lives boldly that many people will find strange, exceptional and odd.

Talk about a variety of ways to put faith into action. Many agencies work in the UK and around the world to help and support others, based on the Christian belief that we are called to serve. Some of those organisations and workers face huge challenges. Where possible, try to communicate the work of mission agencies and individuals to the boys, helping them understand that the Christian faith is not a passive one. If we follow Jesus, we are called to do all we can to bring hope, change and redemption to God's created world. Many agencies have speakers who are available to come and talk through what they do, and it will be helpful to boys to hear an energetic man doing this. Some organisations also provide short-term service opportunities for older teenagers and people in their early 20s, and they can be inspirational to younger boys.

If we are to help the boys in our churches grow successfully into Christian men, we need to include them in the activities of the church from the earliest point on. As I said earlier, many of us will be familiar with the Jesuits' maxim, 'Give me the boy until he is seven, and I will give you the man.' There is a great deal of truth in this. If we accept some of the information above about how boys' brains develop and when testosterone kicks in, making boys behave differently from girls, we have to recognise that we must start including them at an earlier age.

CHAPTER 4

PRAYER WITH BOYS

Prayer is a vital part of our worship and praise. We use prayer to say 'thank you' to God, to express our love and to communicate our desires, as well as making time to listen and be quiet. Often, however, our prayers become a time of begging for things, or trying to 'persuade' God to give us them, rather than an inspirational and meaningful experience.

Prayer is also a vital part of the relationship between God and the boys we work with. It is essential that boys develop an ability to pray both in church worship and in church groups, and that they learn the discipline to develop a personal prayer life. From their experience of church worship, examples of prayer are likely to be passive, with prayers being spoken by someone at the front or written down to be recited by the congregation together. Boys may struggle to read the words, may not connect well with the meaning, and may feel excluded by the way prayers are led. As boys are unlikely to pray openly in a group setting unless they are particularly confident, the use of 'open prayer' may need to be nurtured and encouraged gently. Boys may be embarrassed to share about their personal prayer lives unless it becomes entirely the norm for them and all in the group to do so.

As well as finding the passivity of prayer alien and difficult, boys may also have some cognitive issues about the process of prayer. Boys are more likely than girls to try to rationalise their relationship and communication with God through their logical understanding, and this simply doesn't work. They may be asking questions like, 'How can God possibly hear all of us when we pray?' and 'How can God do all these things?' With boys, we need to keep returning to God's supernatural power, which is so vast that we can't describe or imagine it. God is the ultimate superhero who has never been and can never be defeated, and he has the power to hear our prayers and to answer them in ways that we will never be able to get our heads around.

PRAYER IN CHURCH

To encourage boys to understand and take part in prayer in church, a number of things need to be done.

It's best to make prayer times short and frequent rather than having one long period of prayer. The experience of many worshippers is that a leader, or a volunteer on the prayer rota, enjoys the opportunity to deliver eloquent and complicated prayers that would be a delight in a literary recital event but soon lose the interest of the congregation. Boys will quickly get bored and behave as boys naturally do, when the prayers are too long.

It is also good to vary the voices heard during prayer times. Research shows that we all concentrate better when we hear more than one voice communicating information, as it keeps us engaged and stimulated. It can help boys to keep concentrating if the voices leading or speaking out the prayers come from different places in the church. The variety of voices offered—male and female, younger and older—will also help.

If liturgy is being used, make sure that the response expected from the boys and the wider congregation is clear, accessible and repetitive. If the response changes frequently, boys will disengage. Here are some examples that could be used to begin a service:

We are here, young and old,
We are here to worship God.
We are here, happy and sad,
We are here to worship God.
We are here, male and female,
We are here to worship God.
We are here; all are God's people,
We are here to worship God.

From our homes and our families
We have come together today.
From all that fills our minds
We have come together today.
From the pressures and the problems
We have come together today.
From the happiness and the sadness
We have come together today.

When such 'bidding' prayers are used, there is no reason why a boy or group of boys should not be invited to say the first line, inviting everyone else to join in with the response. Obviously, not all boys would want to do this, and others would need some coaching to help them set the right speed and speak loudly enough for the congregation to hear, but this small level of involvement will help boys keep in tune with both the value and purpose of the prayers.

The written prayers in some denominations' forms of

service can be rather heavy, using words that are not easily understood, even by many adults. There are times when it is appropriate, gently and without ruining the flow of the service and the worship, to explain what a phrase, sentence or passage means. Provide help and support for boys if written prayers and litanies are being followed. Encourage them to listen out for key words, make the words available for them to follow, or insert a regular response.

Where possible, seek out alternative prayers, or write some that include words and concepts that boys will understand. Some denominations are bound to a certain extent in their services by what is regulated, approved or laid down for use. With some creativity and experimentation, though, a lot can be done to help boys engage with the language.

Ensure that those who have planned and are leading the service have thought about how to engage boys in the prayers. This could be done simply by thinking of a physical sign or gesture to make during the prayers. Examples would be:

- Turning round and facing the rear of the church to think about the past and to confess failures and sins over the past few days.
- Turning to the sides of the church to pray for people outside the church, those across the world in difficulties, and people in the community.
- Facing the front to pray for ourselves, our own personal walk with God, and the future of the church family and community.
- Opening hands to receive from God and remember all the blessings that God has given us.

- Pointing thumbs down to think through all the tough situations in the world, the hard times that we or our loved ones are going through, and the darkness of evil in God's world.

- Turning thumbs up to invite the power of the Holy Spirit to be with us and to help us in all we do to serve him.

Some leaders who work with boys find that using a 'prayer drill' or insisting on 'hands together, eyes closed' can be a helpful way of getting boys to stop and concentrate. There are various forms of 'prayer drill', all of which end with hands being held together and eyes closed. One is to open the arms wide, bring the hands together, and then close the eyes. Of course, there is always a temptation for boys to peep and have a look around, but at least some of them will be still and quiet.

Remembering that some boys learn best in a visual way, we can take advantage of the development of new technologies. With an increasing number of churches now using data projection to help with worship, there are many good visual images that can be used to give boys, and others, something to look at during prayers. They include flickering candles, sunsets, people worshipping, the cross, and so on. In a church with many adults, we need to make sure that boys can see the images clearly and are encouraged to look at them during the prayer time.

Work with boys to write prayers that they can use in the church service, offering limited guidance on the structure and not too much help on the content. Allow the boys to pray about things that are important to them. Make sure that those who read the prayers are confident and willing to do so, as not all boys will find it easy. Do avoid the embarrassing situation in which a whole family is invited to lead the prayers at an all-age service, and the boy is required to read out a prayer that his mother has written for him.

Set up prayer activities or 'stations' for boys and men to do alongside girls and women. (There is more about prayer stations later in this book.) When the prayer time comes, ask all the boys to find at least one man to go with them around the activities, and the girls to find at least one woman to do likewise. This allows boys to get to know some of the men in the church, and the adults are encouraged to take an active part rather than resorting to the usual passivity of church prayer.

Even without prayer stations, simple activities can be done alongside some prayers. For instance, many churches will have a formal or informal time of confession, during which the congregation is invited to repent, saying 'sorry' to God. Each person can be given a small piece of paper. While the words are being said, they can screw up the paper and throw it into the aisle or into a bin bag as a sign of giving all the bad things to God and starting afresh. Boys will connect with the activity, and will be particularly engaged if asked to take the bin bag around.

Encourage boys to whisper a short prayer to God when they enter and leave the church worship space. It need only be a few words and should be memorable. This helps them to make prayer a natural thing to do, as well as reinforcing the idea that the church is a special place where we can meet and worship God. Here are some examples of short prayers:

- Be with me here, God.
- God is with us; God is with me.

- You walk with me.

- Jesus is alongside me here.

Invite people from the congregation to speak out things for which they want prayer. Most boys will not be willing to share in this way openly, but the activity and spontaneity will help them see that prayer is a living and active thing, not just about dry words and dull concepts.

Prayer in children's groups and sessions

Prayer should be an integral part of what we do in our groups. Try to avoid being so busy with an active and lively programme that prayer gets squeezed out, sidelined or rushed. The importance of prayer will necessarily make us think about the behaviour we are willing to tolerate when prayer is taking place. Prayers with children should be short and simple, and speech should be clear.

LEADING WITH A PRAYER

Leaders carry some responsibility to set an example and establish prayer as a normal part of what is done in the group and in each session, whatever else may be on the agenda. Ensure that all leaders present take prayer seriously, setting a positive example. If leaders don't participate in prayers, it will be noticed by some boys and will give a negative message. If one leader says a simple, clear prayer as the children arrive for the group, it will not only show boys that prayer is natural, but will also set the right tone for the session.

Use a simple prayer that can be said, whispered or shouted at the beginning and end of the session each time you meet, and becomes familiar to the boys—for example, 'We are all your children, and you are our God. Thank you, God, that we are here as your people. Please be with us today. Help us in all that we do to discover and learn more about you.'

End the led prayers with a response that everyone can join in with. For example, some groups have different ways of saying 'Amen'. Try asking everyone present to wind their arms round and round and get louder as they say 'Ahhhhh', then shout and raise their arms for the 'men' bit. Alternatively, the whole group might bend their knees for the prayer and jump up for 'Amen'. Another approach is to say 'Amen' three times at the end of each prayer, getting louder each time or quieter each time. Some children's groups say 'I agree' or a similar phrase instead of 'Amen', to help children understand what the word means. Boys will enjoy the louder and more physical alternatives to simply saying the word.

Choose a particular space or area in your room to be the prayer space. It doesn't need to have anything specially laid out or put up to identify it, but it will help boys to know what to expect and what is expected of them when you go to that area.

WRITING AND SAYING THEIR OWN PRAYERS

Boys who have a degree of confidence may be willing to write prayers and share them with others in the group or read out prayers that they are familiar with. Other boys will be reluctant to write or read, and many will have some difficulty in doing so. If this is the case, it is important not to put them 'on the spot' or make them feel inadequate or embarrassed. The language used in the prayers needs to be 'despiritualised' so that boys have the confidence to pray out loud without feeling the pressure of getting the language right. The more the group members can be encouraged to write or think of their own prayers, the more likely it is to become habit-forming.

Encourage boys to write short, one-line prayers on different subjects, perhaps giving them the first few words to help them get started. For example:

- Prayers of praise, beginning, 'God, you are awesome because…'

- Prayers of thanks, beginning, 'Thank you, God, that you…'

- Prayers of request, beginning, 'God, you help us all; please help…'

- Prayers of repentance, beginning, 'God, I am really sorry that/for…'

- Prayers of hope, beginning, 'You promise good things; please…'

Stand or sit with the boys in a circle, and ask each one in turn to speak out their prayer. Once the writing of short prayers is established, move on to encourage the boys to work in small groups, making up longer prayers to be said and used regularly within the group.

As an alternative to writing, give boys a sheet of paper and ask them to draw on one side all the things they want to thank God for, and on the other side the things, situations and people that they want to pray for. Then look at some of the drawings with the whole group, exploring the issues and being silent for a short while afterwards for reflection.

OPEN PRAYER

In order to pray openly, boys need to have both confidence in themselves and trust in the group they are with, and these qualities will not develop overnight. For those who feel able, though, there is something very special and important in encouraging boys to speak out their prayers, however short or faltering they may be. Plan a short time within the session where you can have some open prayer, and where the boys can simply sit still and reflect.

Talk with the boys about the importance of silence. Encourage them to be quiet and pray silently in their own minds if they do not want to speak out loud. To break the 'coldness' of silence, you could have a worship CD or other very quiet music playing in the background, appropriate to the mood you are creating.

For those boys who struggle to keep quiet with their eyes closed, provide some pictures or images, or light a candle at a safe distance for them to look at while others have their eyes closed. In order to prevent fidgeting and to demonstrate that this is a time to offer prayer and to receive from God, encourage boys to hold their hands open in front of them during the prayers.

Begin with one or two leaders saying very short prayers, showing how easy it is. Help the boys by giving them something to pray about. You could say, for example, 'Now we need someone to pray for the minister's wife, who is unwell.'

Ask the boys to make their own suggestions of things that need prayer. Much of what they say will be based on the issues the world is facing and things they have seen on the news, and some prayers will be about more personal and family matters. Make a list on a large piece of paper or flipchart and place it where everyone can see it. Invite the boys to glance at it to remind themselves of what needs praying for.

Keep repeating this short activity every time you meet, whether it works really well or whether it fails. It is really important that you don't give up on it.

There may be moments in the programme when something is mentioned or an issue or problem arises, and it is natural simply to stop for a moment and invite a boy to pray a brief prayer about what has happened. This may prove to be a very effective way to demonstrate that prayer is a normal, 'everyday' thing to do and that anyone can pray at any time.

THE LORD'S PRAYER

The Lord's Prayer was taught by Jesus (Luke 11:1-4; Matthew 6:9–13) and has altered little over the 2000 years since. This prayer says it all, and it is worth taking it apart and explaining each section (as suggested for the Apostles' Creed in the previous chapter). Most boys will be at least vaguely familiar with the more modern version of the prayer, as follows:

Our Father in heaven,
hallowed be your name.
Your kingdom come,
your will be done,
on earth as in heaven.
Give us today our daily bread.
Forgive us our sins,
as we forgive those who sin against us.
Lead us not into temptation,

but deliver us from evil.
For the kingdom, the power and the glory are yours,
now and for ever. Amen

Explain to the group that this is called the Lord's Prayer because the Lord Jesus taught it to his followers. He told them to pray using very similar words in their own language to the words we now use.

Break the prayer up into the six sections or 'petitions', and talk briefly about them from a boy's perspective.

PART 1

Our Father in heaven,
hallowed be your name.

Share about who your heroes were when you were younger and who they are now. Who are the boys' heroes? Which sports players, film superheroes and pop musicians do they think are simply great? Explain that nothing and no one can ever come close to the God we worship, who created everything and whose name has amazing power, beyond our imaginations.

PART 2

Your kingdom come,
your will be done,
on earth as in heaven.

Talk with the boys about what they plan for their lives. Explore with them the idea that God cares so much for everyone on earth and the earth itself that he has a plan for them. As we pray that God's 'will' will take place on earth, we are asking God to sort out the very best plan for us and for our lives. Nothing could possibly be better than God's plan for us. Of course, letting God plan our lives seems to take away some of our control, but God gives us free will to make choices, and he wants us to make the best, bravest and strongest choices.

PART 3

Give us today our daily bread.

Talk about food: this is usually a popular subject with boys. Discuss favourite meals, what we celebrate when we have special meals together with friends and family, and what would happen if we didn't have any or enough food. God cares about the little details of our lives as well as the massive things about the world and heaven, and provides us with all that we need.

PART 4

Forgive us our sins,
as we forgive those who sin against us.

Ask who is up for a tough challenge that is only for the brave. Forgiveness is a really huge challenge, yet God shows us again and again that when we do things that are wrong and we feel guilty, God is able to forgive us and give us a fresh start. He allows us to try again and to try harder. If God does that for us, we should do the same for others, however much it hurts and however hard it is.

PART 5

Lead us not into temptation,
but deliver us from evil.

What do boys find tempting? What would tempt them to do something that they know they should not do? Talk through with them the things you are able to share that you find tempting, and what it means for God to protect us from those temptations, which can lead to bad decisions and situations. God is always with us and is willing to guide us away from tempting things. All we need to do is to be strong enough to ignore them. You may want to include some discussion about the huge temptations that Jesus himself faced (Matthew 4:1–10).

PART 6

For the kingdom, the power and the glory are yours,
now and for ever. Amen

Talk about how the Lord's Prayer ends where it began, recognising how great God is and how he has power over everything in the world and beyond. Boys may think they are superheroes and will live for ever in this life, but God promises better than that—a new life for all who love and worship him. That new life, like the power and glory of God, will never end.

Encourage boys to learn the Lord's Prayer so that they can recite it off by heart. When things get tough in their lives, now and in the future, it will prove to be a good foundation. Have a modern version of the Lord's Prayer in clear print on the wall of the space that you use, so that boys who have not learned or remembered it can have a go at reading it.

With the help of suitably skilled musicians, you could teach the boys a sung version of the Lord's Prayer from the many versions available. Boys are not always keen to sing, but there are strategies to help them.

Work with the boys on updating each line, using words and language that they understand and relate to. Over a period of weeks or months, the group could develop a complete, unique version of the prayer that is theirs to use and connects with their experience.

PRAYER RESPONSES

We have already explored this area a little in terms of prayer within the main church worship, and many of those suggestions can also be used in children's groups. Boys may be confident enough, in time, to make up new responses and share them with their peers.

SILENT PRAYERS

Although it could be a bit of a challenge, in the noisy and busy world in which our boys live, it can be very helpful for them to learn to be silent and both listen to their own thoughts and listen to God. Elijah and Jesus are two examples of biblical characters who found God in quietness rather than in words or noise. Quietness can help us all to listen to what God is saying to us.

Explain how many people in the Bible needed to take time away from the normal pressures of life and allow God to speak to them through quietness. Say that, in our imaginations, that is what we are all going to do now. Talk about how God likes us to be quiet to listen to him, as well as speaking and singing, and silence is not something to be worried about.

Provide a focus for boys to look at if they don't want to close their eyes, and make the experience a bit more accessible to boys who are used to noise by having some appropriate quiet music playing.

Invite the boys to imagine that they are sitting quietly on their own in a park, on a hillside, or on a beach near the sea. Lead them in listening to and thinking of God. They may find it helpful to focus on a few questions:

- What do you think God looks like?

- If Jesus were sitting next to you right now, what would you say to him?

- What do you think Jesus would say to you?

Explain that God may want to speak to us through thoughts that pop into our heads, words we hear inside us, and the way we feel. Go on to talk about how some people, when they are praying, see pictures and 'short films' in their minds that are from God.

End the time of quietness with the simple question, 'Does anyone think that God was saying something to them today?' Boys will be encouraged and given confidence to share what they have felt if a leader is willing to get the ball rolling by sharing something simple first.

PRAYING WITH SIGNS AND ACTIONS

Many people are now getting skilled in sign language. Used wisely and sparingly, it is a very powerful and effective tool in worship. Signs and actions have a particular role to play in sung worship, as we will see. It is relatively easy to learn a few of the 'official' signs of Makaton or BSL, and there is nothing to stop you inventing simple signs to accompany prayer. Simple signs can then be tied together to make a visual rather than said or silent prayer. For instance, the response, 'Thank you, God, for loving me' is simple enough for children to learn quickly and remember well. You or the boys could invent signs to go with other simple phrases. For boys, the power of physically communicating our love for God helps them engage with prayer in a fresh way.

BIBLE READINGS AS PRAYER

The Bible contains many passages that are good to read out during a quiet time of reflection, and some are prayers in themselves. Many of the psalms are suitable for reading, and some, such as Psalm 136, have a response that all the boys can join in with. Reading a short account of something amazing that Jesus did during a prayer time can also be helpful, to remind boys of his power and strength.

INTERCESSION

For boys who can be a little self-centred, it's helpful to be reminded to think about and pray for situations and people other than themselves. While they yearn to succeed and do well, they need to be reminded of those who do not have the same opportunities. Through intercession, we bring our requests to God with a firm belief that he hears and answers.

Put up a whiteboard or flipchart in an accessible area and provide marker pens so that the boys can write up things they think should be prayed about. You could bring in a small selection of newspapers from time to time, and ask the boys to rip or cut out the stories that have caught their eye, which they think need prayer.

Invite each boy to say one thing they would like to be prayed about, without putting pressure on boys who do not feel able or willing to make a suggestion. Invite boys to think about their friends who are having tough times, or pray through lists of friends they would like to invite to church or to get involved in your group. There is a great deal of faith-building encouragement to be gained when these sorts of focused prayers are answered. If the group raises money for a particular child, charity or campaign, don't forget to encourage the boys to pray for it.

Before praying, remind the boys of the incredible and amazing power of God to answer prayers and bring change to the people and situations you are praying for. Try to limit the intercessions with the group, to prevent it from becoming a long and tedious 'shopping list' of demands.

Personal prayer life

Boys, as well as all of us who seek to follow Christ, need to get into the habit of praying in their homes and as part of their daily routines. It is not easy, as church leaders, to make sure that this habit develops, as we are limited in what we can do and are reliant to some extent on the importance that parents and carers place on prayer.

Explain to the boys that God is like a best friend, and so much more. Talk about how we spend time with a best friend, and without that time together to talk and laugh, the relationship becomes weaker and we are no longer the great friends that we once were. It's the same in our relationship with God. We need to keep talking to God and listening to him so that the relationship can continue to grow.

Leaders should be encouraged to share appropriate details about how, where and what they pray at home and in other areas of their life outside church. Boys are more likely to pray at home in a regular pattern if they hear that you do, and if they see God working in your life through your prayers.

Ask an older, respected young man from the congregation,

who is familiar to the boys and a positive role model, to come and talk about how they pray personally, why prayer is important to them, and what they learn from listening and being close to God.

Meet with parents and carers to talk about prayer in the home, and particularly the importance of encouraging boys to pray. Remind them that prayer doesn't have to happen at the end of the day while kneeling by the bed, and it doesn't have to be silent or passive. Boys can pray while running around, getting ready for school or playing in the garden and making lots of noise. (Boys particularly like the idea of praying on the toilet!)

Provide boys with a simple prayer to say at the beginning of each day, and another one to say at the end of the day. Print out the prayers on the two sides of a small piece of card, and have plenty of spares available. Here is an example of each:

Thank you, God, for this new day. Thank you, Jesus, that you go with me today. I pray that you will help me in all the things I do.

Thank you, God, for the day I have had. Thank you, Jesus, that you have been with me and helped me. I pray for all the people I have met.

Encourage the boys to set a specific time aside every day to spend five minutes quietly thinking about God and praying in their own way. Ask each boy to tell both you and their parents or carers the prayer time they have chosen, and occasionally ask them whether they are praying and whether they have chosen a good time to do it.

Ask the group as a matter of course whether anyone wants to talk about what they have been praying about at home, and what they feel God has been saying to them. You may not get an answer often, but it reminds the boys that prayer at home is important.

GOD ANSWERS PRAYERS

If we believe that God is like a good parent who only wants to give us good things, then we should be confident in our prayers and sure that God will answer. So we should encourage the boys and the girls we work with to be expectant people, waiting for God to answer the prayers they offer to him. We should also be keen to share those answered prayers with others.

Explore with the group the difficulties that can arise if we expect God to answer in the way we want rather than as part of his plan. For example, the death of a loved one can be especially problematic, if we have prayed for and expected God's answer to be healing and, instead, God's plan has been for the person to have a new eternal life.

Be open about what you have been praying for, and what God has done about it so far, and about things you have been praying for over a long period of time. Ask the boys whether they have seen God answer prayers during the time since the last session, and what God has done. Be natural when talking about answers to prayer, helping them to expect God to work through prayer, despite the fact that none of us can fully understand why and how God answers prayer.

ACTIVE PRAYER IDEAS AND PRAYER STATIONS

Prayer with boys needs to be practical and integral to the programme you have planned. Encouraging boys to write down prayer needs rather than saying them, to speak, whisper or even shout out all together rather than as a lone voice, and to see, touch and do things in prayer will all help. Many boys will respond to opportunities to pray privately, so multisensory prayer stations could be made available for boys to use freely. Make sure there are things to listen to, look at and touch, and that leaders are around to show boys what to do and to gently encourage participation.

Boys relate well to action as much in prayer as they do in anything else. The following selection of ideas is not exhaustive and is not only suitable for boys, but it does focus on the active and the physical. Many of these stations can be set up in church for the whole congregation or in the space where the children's group meets, and can provide opportunities for the children (and adults) to move freely from one to the other. Some of the activities are to be done with the whole group of boys.

JUMP FOR JESUS
Have all the boys standing, and invite some leaders to pray for the group and give thanks for Jesus and his love for us. Every time 'Jesus' is mentioned, the boys should all jump in the air, then settle and listen carefully for the next mention of his name.

CIRCLE PRAYER
Sit all the boys in a circle. Pass round an object (it could be a fun item, such as a foam brick or rubber duck), and let it rest with each boy for 15 seconds. In that time, the boy holding the object is free to speak out a word or two about God.

BOUNCE TO BOYS

Stand the boys in a circle and give them a large, soft foam ball. Each one should say, 'I pray for…' and then bounce the ball to the person they have named. That boy does the same to someone else, and so on. Once the ball has been bounced to all the boys at least once, pause and spend a short time in silence while the boys think of and pray for those they named.

FLYING PRAYERS

You will need a parachute, play canopy or large bedsheet. Ask the boys to write one or two words about things they want to pray about, or people who need prayer, on to small pieces of paper. Then stand around the parachute, raise and wave it, and throw the pieces of paper into the middle. Then lift it as high as possible so that the pieces of paper fall off. Each boy should then pick one up, read it and silently pray about the things written on it. Everyone then returns to the parachute to repeat the process.

THANK YOU, GOD…

The song 'Thank you, God, for this fine day' is well known and popular, and so simple that it does not need a musician to lead it. Start singing it, with the boys joining in, and then point to one boy, indicating that he should say what he would like to thank God for. If you do this quickly, children will not have time to get nervous or worried and will respond with whatever is on their minds. It can be repeated many times

STAR PRAYERS

Boys like doing star prayers, especially if they are in a mixed group. Star prayers offer an intimacy that helps boys open up and speak out. Each small group of four or five boys should lie on the floor, face down, with their heads close together in a circle and their bodies spanned out like a star. If you have enough male leaders, place a leader with each group. Encourage the boys to talk about God and to pray in their star-shapes.

GLOBE PRAYERS

Make a few inflatable globes available. Encourage the boys to pick one up, throw it up in the air, and then look closely at the first country they see when they catch it. They should then stand and think about that country and pray for it for a few moments.

STOP AND TEASPOON

Try either of these tried-and-tested methods to facilitate prayer times with the children.

Using the word STOP, focus on each letter and what it represents:

- **S for Sorry:** Invite the boys to silently or quietly say something they have done recently that they feel sorry about.

- **T for Thank You:** Invite them to think of the good things they have in life and to say some of them quietly.

- **O for Others:** Ask the boys to think of at least one person they know who they want to pray for, and to say the name after you have counted to three.

- **P for Please:** Encourage the boys to be silent for a few moments and think about the things they need to receive from God.

You can follow the same pattern with the letters T, S and P from 'teaspoon' (Thank you, Sorry and Please). Plastic teaspoons are cheap to buy, and they could be used to enhance this prayer activity and to encourage TSP praying at home.

JIGSAW PRAYERS

Find on the internet or in newspapers five different pictures that clearly show people or situations that need prayer—for example, homeless people, people who are ill, or sad children. If you have a large group, you may need more pictures. Mount each image on to different coloured paper or light card. Then cut the cards randomly into five pieces.

Hide four of the five pieces around the room, give each pair or small group of boys the one remaining piece of a picture, and ask them to search for the other pieces. Once they have found the pieces, they should sit and put the picture together, work out what it shows, and then pray silently or aloud about it.

JIGSAW PRAYERS AS A PRAYER STATION

For individual prayers, place the jigsaw pieces in an area where the boys can sit, put them together, and pray quietly on their own for the situations the images represent.

PRAYER WALL

Cover a wall with paper and provide marker pens so that the boys can write up names of people who need prayer, situations that have been in the news, and answers to prayer. It is possible to purchase rolls of paper with a 'wall' pattern printed on them.

PRAYER TREE

Set up a large house plant with branches, a large branch of a tree, or a Christmas tree. Invite the boys to write simple prayers on luggage labels and tie them on to the branches.

DRAWING PRAYERS

Provide paper and pens or pencils, and invite the boys to draw things and people they want to pray for. Those drawings can then be put up on a board for others to see and think about.

PILE THE STONES

Make a pile of clean stones in a quiet space with the simple prayer, 'God, I walk with you on my journey through life' on display next to it. Place a bag of stones a few steps away. Explain to the boys that, in Old Testament times, people placed stones in a small pile, as a marker that they had been there and that God was with them. Even today, on mountain paths, small piles called 'cairns' are built to mark the way and to show that others have journeyed past that spot. Invite the boys to mark that they are on their journey of life and want God to be with them, by taking a stone, walking to the pile and placing it on top. They can stand in front of the pile and say the prayer quietly and individually.

WASHING HANDS

Place a bowl of water and some cloths, or wet wipes, in an area of the room. Invite the boys to go to that space individually and wash their hands, remembering that God is kind and willingly forgives all the wrong things they have done.

WOOL WEB

Have all the boys standing in small circles of no less than four and no more than eight in each. Give one person in each circle a ball of wool, and invite them to hold the end of the wool and throw the ball to someone else, saying that person's name as they do so. The next person holds the thread in one hand while throwing the ball to someone else, naming them at the same time. This is repeated until everyone has been thrown the ball of wool at least once.

Then stop and ask for silence. Ask each person to look along one thread from their hand and pray for the person it leads to. Then ask them to do the same following a second thread, and so on. The connections between people and the sense of being united makes this a very special prayer activity.

TO THE LIGHT

Place a lit candle on a low table or, if you think this may be too risky, use a battery-operated candle. Ask the boys to think of bad, sad, dark things that they know about or that are in their lives. Explain that the light of Jesus can take away all darkness, and ask them to sit quietly for a minute or two, looking at the light.

LIGHT OF THE WORLD

Holding a large lit candle, explain that you are all going to be silent for two minutes to think about the people, places and situations in the world that need the light of Jesus to be with them. Begin and end the time with the boys repeating after you, 'Jesus is the light of the world.' During a two-minute silence, invite the boys to look at the lit candle and think about all the light that Jesus brings to dark things.

COLOURS OF GOD'S CREATION

Inflate some balloons, at least as many as there are boys in your group. Throw them into the air and ask each boy to catch one and think of one thing in God's creation that is the same colour as the balloon. Then say, 'God, we thank you that you made...', at which point all the boys can shout out their ideas together.

WORDS FOR GOD

Inflate some balloons. Explain that you are going to throw them into the air, and the group must not let them fall to the floor. Each time a balloon comes near them, each person should tap it back up into the air and, as they do so, speak or shout out one word to describe God. You could give a few ideas to get them started: amazing, wonderful, incredible, almighty, strong, powerful, and so on.

BUBBLE PRAYERS

Praying with bubbles is similar to the use of incense in some churches. Prayers are sent to God and, as bubbles float upwards, they represent our prayers. You can use large bubble machines or smaller 'toy' bubble machines that are battery-powered, or you can provide small pots of bubbles for individuals to use. As they see the bubbles rising, the boys should be encouraged to imagine people's faces or situations that need prayer, and think about them while they watch the bubbles float away.

EXERCISE PRAYERS

Lead a short time of prayer while the boys (and adult leaders, to set the example) do the following exercises:

- Lie on the floor: thank God for times of rest and peace.

- Stand and make a big circle with arms outstretched: thank God for the world and his creation.

- Run on the spot: pray for the things that we need to do.

- Touch knees: pray about the times when life is tough and we feel tired.

- Climb a mountain on the spot: pray for other people struggling and in difficulty.

- Star jumps: pray that we will all reach out and help others.

There are many more possible exercise combinations that boys will really enjoy doing.

PAST, PRESENT, FUTURE, OURSELVES

Label each wall of the room with one of the following four words. When you say each word, the boys should run to the wall with that label, pause and pray or stand silently thinking about the subject, in the terms suggested below.

- Past (repentance, pain and guilt, forgiveness).

- Present (those we know and love, the church, the world and our community).

- Future (our hopes and plans, mission to reach more people for Christ, the hope for peace).

- Ourselves (what we can say to God, and what he may be saying to us).

PUPPETS

Puppets can be great communication aids, and many boys relate well to them. For younger boys, you can use a puppet to lead prayers, asking them what they think the puppet should be praying about. Boys are, remarkably, more likely to tell the puppet about their issues for prayer than they are to tell an adult.

QUICK TRIPLETS

Give each boy a subject for prayer written on a small piece of paper. Subjects could include 'Those who are ill', 'Our schools', 'Our church', and so on. Ask the boys to walk, run, hop, crawl or otherwise move around freely. When you shout 'Triplets' they have to find two other boys and sit on the floor in their triplets. They then have 30 seconds to read their three papers and pray about those subjects. Most boys will pray silently, but, as the activity is quick and energetic, some will feel confident to say a few words.

ALL TOGETHER

Begin by talking about any people in the church community who are ill or in special need of prayer. Then ask the boys if they have any suggestions. Say a simple bidding such as 'God, we pray for...' and encourage the children to speak or shout out the names of people who need prayer, all at once. This activity works best once the boys have got used to the idea and have gained confidence. It could be extended so that boys say whole prayers individually, but at the same time.

PICK AND MIX

Ask the boys to work in pairs or small groups to write, on small slips of paper, things that they think should be prayed about. As they do so, give them some guidance, aiming for a mixture of topical and general issues. Place the papers face down on a table or put them in a hat. Allow the boys to take one at a time and pray for that subject silently before putting the paper back and taking another one.

PRAYER RUN

If this is possible occasionally, take the boys for a short run or jog around the community and neighbourhood of the church, and stop at some of the points suggested to pause, be quiet, and pray or reflect.

- **Shops:** Remember that God provides for us. Perhaps we have everything we need, or perhaps not. Some people are poor and can't buy things easily.

- **Houses:** Pray for people in the community who may be elderly or lonely, or have big decisions to make or families to look after, and so on. Ask God to be with them all, whatever their needs are.

- **Park or open ground:** Thank God for his natural creation and the good things of grass, trees, fields, mountains and streams.

- **School:** Pray for the children and young people in the area, that more of them would learn about God and come to know him, and that they would be safe.

- **Care home:** Pray for older people, giving thanks for their wisdom and knowledge and asking God to bring them peace and healing.

- **Industrial buildings:** Ask God to be with the workers here and everyone who works. Pray for those who don't enjoy their work, and those who are trying to find employment.

CHAPTER 5

WORSHIP WITH BOYS IN CHILDREN'S GROUPS

Boys may be comfortable to sing, shout and chant when they are with men (mostly) on football terraces or rugby grounds. There, they seem far less inhibited in making their voices heard as they chant raucously and sing loudly the first few phrases of songs. When we consider sung worship in our children's groups, we have a number of problems that churches need to think through. The basic components of worship are likely to be prayer and songs, but boys are not always keen to sing, and it can be a real struggle if you don't have musicians to lead the worship.

However, music touches all of us and connects us with 'something other'. Many of us will have seen how even young babies can be startled, excited or transfixed by music, and, as adults, we often hear songs that remind us strongly of occasions or incidents in our past.

Singing is great fun. Many children—even many boys, with the right modelling and encouragement—enjoy singing and even making up their own songs and tunes. Adults enjoy singing too, but many of us reserve it for the shower or for the car when we are driving alone.

Making music by singing and playing instruments can help boys to develop basic and fine motor skills, which girls generally find easier naturally. When boys clap different rhythms, shake shakers or tap drums, they are physically engaged and active. Boys with the special needs we have already considered may find singing to be soothing and calming. Professionals use music therapy to help children with special needs to connect with themselves and the world around them. For boys, learning a new song can give them both a personal sense of achievement and the all-important feeling that they are united with others in their peer group. Nothing unites quite as well as making music together.

Singing in worship can help boys to express what they think and feel about their faith without having to stand out from the crowd and verbalise what God means to them. Here are some helpful guidelines:

- Make singing part of being in God's family. Our boys need to get into the habit of singing worship to God as people have done, way back into Old Testament times. You should explain this from time to time, so that they understand the importance of worship through song. Sung worship should not simply be a time-filler.

- Choose songs carefully to ensure that some are 'boy-friendly'. Boys are likely to be helped by and to connect with songs about challenge, battle, strength, heroes, risk and journey. They may not relate so well to songs about love, gentleness, kindness, submission and surrender to God, even though these are all good spiritual concepts.

- Make sure the words make sense. Young children may not understand fully what they are singing, but, as they learn words and express their love for God, they will also be learning basic words and phrases that will make sense later on. Once children have reached a more sophisticated level of understanding, we have a responsibility to check songs to be sure that they make sense.

- Make sure the words are worth knowing. Some worship songs are fairly meaningless and teach nothing to the singers. Many adults will testify to having formed the basis of their doctrine and theology through the words they sang as children in church. If the worship songs you sing with boys do not teach them anything biblical or anything worth remembering, then use different songs.

- In particular, reject 'silly' songs. Children's worship songs are often lively and involve silly actions that adults and many boys, particularly as they grow older, are very embarrassed to use. This isn't to say that sung worship with boys shouldn't be fun, but being silly for the sake of it is not what worship should be about.

- Teach the meanings. Some boys will not understand the words and concepts in some songs. Without being too heavy about it, you can gently and briefly explain the meaning of the more difficult words and phrases.

- Don't worry about the quality of the singing. Whatever the children offer to God will be real for them at that time and shouldn't be undervalued. To the trained adult ear, the sound may not be enjoyable, and we may be aware that some boys are very poor singers. But God calls us all to worship him, and he delights in our worship whatever it sounds like.

- Don't ask children to 'perform' their worship. Many churches have moved away from the common practice of dragging children to the front to sing a little song to the adult congregation, and rightly so. Children shouldn't be asked to 'perform' in worship any more than adults are. For boys, who may be shy or fear public attention, the 'kiddy slot' can be painfully embarrassing.

- Let the boys choose the songs sometimes. Songs in church go through phases of popularity. If boys connect with a particular song, take advantage of their enthusiasm and use it.

- Introduce a range of songs. It is good to use familiar songs, but, as well as familiarity, children relish a little variety. You should be aiming for a balance each week, carefully introducing new songs from time to time, and reintroducing old ones that have been forgotten. This means that it is important to keep lists.

Leading worship with boys needs careful planning and can be hard work. Boys are likely to enjoy action songs and loud songs, although they are able to worship with quieter songs if they are appropriately led and if there are men showing them how to do it. It's important, therefore, to invest in worship leaders. It saddens me that many churches have talented musicians but no one considers putting them on a rota to lead worship with the children's groups. If we are to encourage boys to sing, it will be helpful if they are led by a talented man from the wider church.

All the leaders, as well as the designated worship leader, need to set an example by demonstrating clearly to the boys that they are engaging fully in the worship, not chatting at the back or doing some clearing up or preparation for the next activity. They need to join in with the actions, sing with enthusiasm, raise their hands or close their eyes as appropriate. If boys see adults not taking worship seriously, they will feel that they can behave similarly. The best leaders are there to model what worship is, not to perform or to disengage.

When leading worship, give boys clear directions. If you want them to stand, hold their hands open, look at a picture or the cross, or anything else, make the instructions really clear so that boys can follow them easily. Also, don't rely on the boys' ability to read words. As we know, many boys do not find it easy to read text. It may be difficult for them to keep up with reading words from a screen, and they may be inhibited if the words are in a book that they must hold. Songs should be led and taught gradually so that boys learn the words and rely on the written lyrics only as a prompt.

When teaching new songs, start with the actions if there are any. Teach them by repetition, and move on to the words only when the actions are clear. (For younger children, avoid too many complex actions.) Teach the words line by line for the children to say, speaking the words and doing the actions to fit the rhythm of the song. Next, sing the song through, encouraging the children to join in with the actions and to start singing when they have picked up the tune. Don't be over-ambitious: boys are likely to pick up a limited number of words at one time, and it may be best to introduce new verses on another occasion. For the reasons mentioned earlier, don't rely on projected words for boys to follow, and remember that the next time you sing the song, some boys will have forgotten most of it.

Do introduce some quiet songs. Boys are helped by

learning and singing quiet songs, as long as there is something for them to do while they sing. It may be something to touch, a particular way to move while they sing, or some images to look at. It is wrong to suggest that boys will only connect with God through exuberant actions and loud noise.

Also, encourage boys to use instruments. There are plenty of small and inexpensive percussion instruments available, and many boys who need to be doing things in worship will find shaking or tapping an instrument really helpful. With careful guidance, they will also learn when not to use the instrument, perhaps during quieter songs, thus enhancing the worship for everyone. Most boys will want to play instruments, so the opportunity to be given one can be used as a positive incentive.

If you are unable to provide live music for leading children in worship, there are many CDs, DVDs and online songs with backing tracks, visuals, actions, words and music that you can use. However, these resources are not easy to stop and start, and they make it difficult to vary the pace or to learn the song by repeating a section at a time. The most versatile instrument is the voice of the leader, and the children will not notice if your singing voice is weak or if you are embarrassed by it. Once you launch into a familiar song, the children will join you quickly, find the pitch and sing along.

Boys need variety and challenge. You can easily make the sung worship session more boy-friendly with a few changes, as follows:

- Work with the boys on writing new words or verses for a familiar song tune. You could use a secular melody or a tune from an existing worship song. Ask them to write something that represents their lives as boys and how they see our great and powerful God. This provides a chance for peer group activity and a sense of success.

- There is a good opportunity to go deeper into worship by missing out all the words for a verse and asking the boys to be quiet and listen to the music alone, raising or holding their hands out or moving slowly around, thinking of what the words of the song mean.

- If there is a word that is used regularly in a particular song, ask the boys to miss it out each time it comes round. The same could be done with actions, making it challenging and fun, especially when the leaders go wrong. Boys will enjoy the challenge and sense of achievement that this gives them.

- Doing the actions without the words can help boys to think through the meaning of what they sing. They will be thinking of the words while doing something physical, but not having to multitask by singing at the same time.

WORSHIP WITHOUT SINGING

There's a great deal you can do in worship that does not rely on singing. Biblically, worship includes dance and movement, responses and chants, and physical demonstrations of our love for God. Boys enjoy the active and physical, so try to incorporate some of these elements from time to time to help them engage.

As we have already considered, actions and signs can be used in prayer and quiet times, as well as with songs. Simple phrases and words can easily be given made-up or 'official' signs, and many boys will enjoy making up signs for words.

Chants and raps can be frightening to leaders, but boys love them and will be used to shouting them on the school playground. Boys will be creative with this sort of thing and will not find it difficult to suggest lines to chant. Here's an easy example:

God you're here,
God you're here,
'Cos you're here, I
have no fear.

Clapping rhythms, as well as using simple percussion instruments, is a good developmental exercise in itself. It helps boys to keep active, which in turn helps them concentrate. You can put simple words and phrases to a rhythm and encourage the boys to speak, shout or chant it. Again, it doesn't take much effort, just a bit of bravado and some energetic boys.

Play quiet worship CDs when you want the children to settle down to reflect and think about God, perhaps when they are preparing to go back into church or to go home. This will calm them and give them a sense of peace and security.

WORSHIP IN A LARGER CONTEXT

If you can arrange it, try to take boys to bigger children's worship events. They will gain a lot from seeing other boys, getting to know about other churches and worshipping loudly at a standard that they may not experience in their own church. Some areas in the UK hold evening worship events called *X:site*, which are resourced and supported by Scripture Union. These events are organised centrally in an area where there are a number of churches, offering worship on a bigger scale for children from a range of churches.

CHAPTER 6

WORSHIP WITH BOYS IN CHURCH

Boys may struggle in church and congregational worship, depending on its style. Unfortunately much of the worship that goes on in churches is static and doesn't involve a great deal of congregational involvement or activity. There is no particular church tradition or denomination that is better or worse for boys in terms of worship: all have positive things to offer and other elements that may need to be reconsidered. The key to keeping boys engaged is to think through some of the basics from a boy's point of view. Are there things to do? Are there activities to take part in? Are there visual aids to look at, that hold their interest? Are there songs that are accessible and fun to sing?

TRADITIONAL WORSHIP

As we know, not all boys conform to our expectations. Very traditional worship has its attractions for some boys, and can be very beneficial for those with particular needs such as autism, who respond well to a sense of order, predictability and ritual. Some boys feel safe in the church environment, knowing that what will happen is what they expect to happen. Boys may be drawn to the more theatrical aspects of traditional worship in the Catholic and Anglo-Catholic style. The formality, ritual and involvement have benefits, including the following:

- **Clear roles to play:** There are roles for boys in traditional worship. With appropriate training, they can be acolytes or altar-servers; they can carry a candle or the cross, be a part of the Gospel procession, sing in the choir, and so on. Having a role keeps boys engaged and committed to church, gives them a sense of belonging, enhances their self-esteem and makes them feel part of something bigger.
- **Ceremonial:** Some boys respond well to the sense of pageantry and ceremony that traditional worship offers. They enjoy watching things happen, and are drawn to the vibrant colours of robes, vestments, altar frontals and decorations.
- **Set routines and patterns:** Those boys who struggle with too much variety will find that set patterns and predictability add security and comfort, and will therefore help them worship.
- **A sense of something 'other':** For boys living in a noisy, complex and challenging world, the entirely different feel of a traditional church and all that it entails can be liberating, helping them connect with God in a fresh way.

Of course, traditional worship does lack the variety, participation and interaction that many boys will be seeking.

ENGAGING BOYS IN CHURCH WORSHIP

Boys need to learn to worship in church, however challenging that might be for them and for the adults in the congregation. There is always a difficult balance to be held when encouraging boys to worship appropriately in a mixed setting: we want them to worship with us, but we don't want to stifle or inhibit their natural boyish behaviour. Here are some helpful pointers:

- Boys like to know what is going to happen. As most worship in our churches is designed for adults, we need to remember that some boys, who may struggle with the inactivity and the reliance on reading, need to know what is coming next and be prepared for it.

- Many boys don't engage with written words. Spend some time looking at the words included in the service, whether liturgy or song lyrics, and consider how they can be reduced.

- Boys like to be involved. Boys will keep coming to church and being part of the worship if they have a job to do or if they can volunteer to do something specific as part of the service. There is a role for boys in making music and contributing to the worship of the church (more of which later).

- Boys need appropriate songs and hymns. We've touched on this in the context of children's group worship, but it is just as relevant for the whole congregation. How should we expect boys and men to respond to the type of worship songs that are sometimes summarised as 'Jesus is my boyfriend'? Churches need to look carefully at the words and concepts we are inviting men and boys to proclaim. While I wouldn't call for a return to Victorian worship, there was some value in vibrant, aspirational and forceful songs such as 'When a knight won his spurs', 'Fight the good fight' and 'Onward, Christian soldiers', which we have lost. Modern worship, in which one mid-tempo song merges with another, with words or tunes that are not properly taught so that the congregation can easily join in, can cause boys to disengage very quickly.

- Boys need help from men. As well as seeing men at the front in leadership roles, boys need to see men worshipping, so that they can be guided by them and copy them. Men have an important role in accompanying boys through worship and demonstrating that men can worship too.

- Boys need interaction. When planning worship where boys are present, we need to limit the length of each section or activity, and provide opportunities for boys to interact with the wider congregation. Some churches 'share the peace', and this can be a good opportunity for some contact across genders and generations. However, when this happens, adults very often ignore the children present.

- Boys need touch, movement and visual stimulation. As we have seen, boys will pray better if they have things to look at, they will learn better if they have something to touch or fiddle with, and they will concentrate better if they have something to look at. Worship needs to include all these elements.

- Boys need each other. Even if children are expected to sit with their parents and carers during a service, it will help boys to feel as if church is a place for them if they are sitting near and have contact with other boys of the same age and older.

- Boys get uncomfortable quickly. This is not a call for the wholesale disposal of hard wooden pews, but it is a reminder that fidgety boys find pews really uncomfortable, and the back of the pew in front looks like a very good thing to kick. We need to be realistic about how long we expect boys to sit, where they sit, and on what they sit.

It's worth noting that some boys will draw attention to themselves. In any worship service, there may be a few boys who try to challenge the leader by misbehaving, giving inappropriate answers to questions, making noises or being otherwise unhelpful. It may not be the leader's responsibility to deal with this sort of behaviour, but, if they have to, the best option is often not to respond at all to the boy or boys involved. When working with children, one of the hardest skills to learn is to know when and when not to respond.

CHAPTER 7

BOYS AND THE BIBLE

It is essential that we help boys to engage with and get excited by the Bible, but it isn't enough simply to hand over a book that has over 1000 pages of text and is split up into other sections with names, chapters, verse numbers, footnotes and lots of difficult words. We need to consider how to communicate the Bible to boys, what they can see about boys in it, and how the Bible presents Jesus to them.

COMMUNICATING THE BIBLE

There are many ways in which you can help to bring the Bible to life for boys. When you are reading Bible passages with them, make sure you use a translation of the Bible with language that boys will understand. Older, more traditional versions may include lovely poetic language, but boys find them difficult to read, and we need to make their reading of the Bible as accessible as possible. If the Bible you use has pictures, show them to the boys so that they can imagine a little better what the scene may have looked like. Stick to short passages of the Bible at any one time, and, if the boys are required to read it themselves, make sure they are not expected to read it out loud on their own.

If you are reading the Bible to the boys, try the following ways of helping them to focus on what they are hearing.

- Read short passages twice over. Ask the boys to listen with their eyes open the first time, and with eyes closed the second time, to help them to visualise the pictures you are describing in the words.

- Introduce deliberate mistakes. Read out a short passage twice, once as it is written, but then with some fairly obvious wrong words thrown in. Boys will enjoy the competition of trying to spot the errors while listening attentively.

- Communicate a short passage of scripture by encouraging the boys to repeat each line after you have read it. Vary the volume—using a loud and soft voice, whispering, and so on.

- Vary the voice you use. If possible, when reading biblical text, use at least two voices so that boys can engage with the variety of the text. Dramatised Bible versions are easily available.

- Dress up in simple costumes. Boys find it easier to learn from and think about a 'third person', which is why puppets work well for many of them. It may be a little embarrassing for a leader to put on a costume, but it will help some boys to listen and connect with the story differently.

- Introduce action verses and memory verses. There are many resources to help you do this. The simplest way to teach a memory verse is to write each word on a separate piece of paper, display and repeat the whole verse, then take words away, one at a time, until the boys can say the whole verse without reading it. Several Christian workers, such as Doug Horley and John Hardwick, produce song DVDs and albums of scripture verses put to music, with actions. These are ideal to help boys learn the Bible through listening, doing and participating with others.

Another way to present the Bible is to use DVDs and clips from social media sites. Boys enjoy looking at things, although you should not use long films or stories. Always make sure you have watched a DVD through first and checked that it is appropriate and helpful in bringing out the message you are hoping to offer.

Many boys enjoy argument, and some have a very strong sense of justice. Give boys an opportunity to think through, argue and debate two sides of a Bible story. An example could be the parable of the lost son, focusing on how the other brother felt when his father welcomed back the prodigal son with such enthusiasm and expense. Once the story has been told, ask one boy to take the part of the older brother, and to put into words how he is feeling and why he thinks he is right. Then allow another to play the part of the father, trying to explain that the return of the younger brother is worth more than anything else. Moderate and keep a check on the boys as they argue it out.

Encourage boys to find their own way around the Bible, too. This can be done helpfully by keeping a list of the books of the Bible clearly visible on the wall of the room you use, or helping, encouraging and actively engaging boys in the use of the contents page at the front of the Bible to discover where to find the different books.

Always have a Bible visible and within reach so that you can refer to it, even if you are telling a story you have learned or are reading a passage from another resource. Preface your reading of a Bible passage with a comment such as, 'And this story comes from the middle of the Bible, just before when Jesus was born', or whatever is appropriate.

You can introduce the whole Bible in small sections—for example, by giving boys a copy of one of the Gospels to look at. Keep reminding them that the word 'Bible' means 'library', so it is a collection of lots of different books, not one huge, scary monster.

Boys' personal Bible reading

Encourage boys to engage with the Bible at home as well as in your church group, perhaps by providing Bible reading notes or similar resources. You could produce some Bible notes of your own, with a short passage to look at and a few questions to consider. Ask boys whether they have read anything from their Bibles over the past few days, and talk openly about what you have read and what it has meant to you. Try to model some active use of the Bible.

Give boys a list of the books of the Bible, in the right order, for them to keep handy and use at home. This will reinforce their use of the contents page in their Bible.

Introduce graphic Bibles and cartoon Bibles. Some are available especially for seasons, such as Christmas and Easter, and others cover the whole span of the Bible. They are designed principally with boys in mind, including good pictures with angular shapes and primary colours pre-dominating, limited text to read, and a degree of clarity and excitement that boys appreciate. As mentioned previously, Scripture Union's *Guardians of Ancora* Bible-based game app is also especially engaging for boys.

Help boys to use the Bible as their moral compass.

Occasionally set them a challenge to go home and find out what the Bible has to say about a particular issue, and bring their discoveries back to the next group meeting. If there's a competitive element (a simple prize on offer, for instance), some boys will enjoy doing this and will gain confidence in using the Bible at the same time.

It's important to engage parents and carers in supporting their boys. Where possible, the main carers should take some responsibility, encouraging boys to read and think about the Bible, reading the Bible to them where appropriate, and discussing Bible stories openly as a family. There are resources in print and on the internet to help families engage better with spiritual and biblical issues in the home. BRF's www.faithinhomes.org.uk is one example.

THE WHOLE BIBLE

Most boys are fascinated by things that are scary, and enjoy a bit of horror, gore and unpleasant stuff. The 'Horrible Histories' series is hugely popular with boys because it focuses on some of the more dramatic aspects of history. Boys also enjoy reading good stories with an element of excitement and risk, but these stories are best delivered in short chunks of text or as cartoons. Most of all, boys need to know about battle—the battles for justice in the Old Testament, the battle to spread the Christian message in the New Testament, and the heroic battle of Jesus.

In order to help boys get a rounded and perhaps more 'masculine' view of scripture and what God may want to say to them through it, we need to help them get to know the entire word of God. Make them aware of some of the more difficult and challenging biblical stories. You will obviously need to prepare carefully to ensure that you deliver the story well and that you can respond to some of the difficult questions that may follow.

When communicating difficult Bible stories, allow plenty of time for boys to follow what is going on. Ask them helpful questions, such as, 'What would you have done in this situation?' and 'Why do you think God did that?'

Also, be honest about how you feel about some of the more difficult stories, including accounts of battles in which thousands are slaughtered, or passages where God seems to be a vengeful rather than forgiving God. Make clear that it is impossible for people to understand everything about God, because God is beyond our human brains. It is really helpful for boys to know that we as leaders don't always have the answers.

Let boys learn about heroic successes and heroic failures. Boys need to identify with heroes who have flaws because, as they grow, they will become disproportionately aware of their own faults and may only see potential failure. Noah remained a hero despite getting drunk and doing some bad things. God made David a success despite his unreliability. All of them, and all of us, have the chance for redemption.

Be aware that many boys have to work hard to empathise with characters in stories, so try to focus as much as possible on what the events meant for the people in the stories.

Of course, all of this has to be done sensitively and with some consideration for the age of the boys, as we don't want to encourage nightmares! On the other hand, we mustn't short-change our boys by giving them the impression that the Bible is a nice book, full of stories about being nice. Many children's Bibles sanitise the Bible, making it too easy, soft and genteel. Many of the materials you have available to use with groups may do this too. For all children but particularly, in this context, for boys, the Bible needs to be presented as a complete document, not one that only contains pleasant stories.

Make sure boys know how the bits of the Bible fit together. As boys are helped by clear directions and information and are attracted to visual stimuli, make sure that they have easy access to a Bible timeline, and refer to it regularly. Point out where the story or passage you are reading fits into the big picture, and how it relates to the coming of Jesus.

Try to introduce some biblical content that is not story-based. For instance, the book of Proverbs includes some real gems, and boys love having a go at making up wise words and phrases. Help boys to understand what the Psalms were for and the contexts within which they were written, and encourage them to write their own words and songs of praise.

Do not be afraid to help boys imagine what the events in the book of Revelation might look like. It would be difficult to use much of Revelation as teaching material, but to read short extracts from some of the most dramatic and fantastic passages, while the boys have their eyes closed, will really fire their imaginations.

Remember, too, that boys are fascinated by how things work, so the biblical miracles may be both a challenge to their understanding and a problem for them, if they can't work out how the miracles happened. They will need some support in thinking through how some of the Old Testament miracles worked and in exploring the theories of how and why God did what he did. There are sometimes possible, though unproven, physical or geological explanations of miracles that boys will enjoy exploring as they consider God's power.

Boys in the Bible

There are plenty of significant boys and men in the Bible, and, to help boys engage, we need to help them find out about those boys and men. There are materials available to help with this, including my book *Bible Heroes* (SU, 2011). The following four examples will help boys to understand that the Bible was written about and for people like them. The questions are offered as a guide to aid discussion about what it means to be a boy and a man for God.

SAMUEL

Many boys will be familiar with the story in 1 Samuel 3 of how God called Samuel, but it is still worth exploring a little further. Samuel was given to God's service by his mother, and he worked as a helper to the priest Eli in the temple. One night, Samuel heard a voice calling his name and ran to Eli to find out what he wanted. Eli told Samuel that he had not called him. This happened a second and a third time until Eli guessed that it could be God's voice that Samuel was hearing, and told him to answer with, 'Speak, Lord, for your servant is listening.' When he heard the voice a fourth time, Samuel did exactly that, and God spoke to him and told him that there was work for him to do.

- Samuel was given to God's work, and his mother prayed for him. Who do you think might be praying for you to know God better?

- When God spoke to Samuel, he got up and ran to Eli, expecting to be given some work. God loves the energy that boys have. Are you willing to use your energy for God?

- God spoke to Samuel even though he was still a young boy, and gave him a big job to do. Could you do more for God in your life, even now?

KING JOASH

King Joash's story is told in 2 Chronicles 24 and 2 Kings 12. He was appointed king when he was around the age of seven, but even before that he had escaped an attempt to capture and murder him. With the support and advice of the priest Jehoiada, Joash did a lot of good things. He managed to raise money to rebuild the temple for worship, and he encouraged total honesty. Joash was young but strong and determined to do what was right, and he did so for as long as he listened to good advice. When Jehoiada died, however, Joash started to go wrong. He listened to the wrong people, failed to do God's work, and was finally killed by a group of his own leaders who turned against him when he was just 33 years old.

- God chooses young men and boys to be leaders. You don't need to be old to do things for God. What do you think God may want you to do?

- God provides people for us to look up to, and to be a support to us. Joash had Jehoiada as his support: who do you look to for a good example?

- Things went wrong when Joash stopped listening to good advice and stopped doing what God wanted. How could he have avoided this?

THE BOY WITH THE FISH AND BREAD

In John 6:1–13 we read that the twelve disciples were getting worried about how to provide enough food for the 5000 people who had been listening to Jesus. Finally, Andrew found a boy who had five small loaves of bread and two fish for his lunch, and these supplies were offered to Jesus. As Jesus prayed and shared the food, it became enough to feed everyone, with plenty left over.

- The boy was the one who was willing to give. Often, boys give a good example to adults about doing the right thing. How could you be a good example?

- The boy handed over his lunch, knowing that others needed it. What could you give to help others?

- We don't know what happened to that boy, but he was really important to God's big plan and the story of Jesus and what he did on earth. Does it matter if we do good things but we ourselves are not remembered for them?

EUTYCHUS

The story of Eutychus is found in Acts 20:7–12. He is described in some translations as a 'young man', and was probably a teenager. Eutychus was among a gathering of people in a room on the third floor of a house, where the heat and fumes from the lamps would have had a sleep-inducing effect. Paul was preaching, and preached 'on and on' until midnight, by which time Eutychus was asleep, leaning on the side of a window. As he slept, he fell from the window and landed on the street below. Paul rushed down, prayed for healing, and the young man recovered.

- Eutychus was in the right place, trying to learn more about Jesus. Even though it may be tough, are you excited to learn more?

- Eutychus wanted to be a real man of God and never gave up wanting more of God in his life. Will you be a man of God?

- As Paul prayed, a miracle happened and Eutychus was made alive and healthy again. Do you believe that those things happened? Do you think miracles can happen today?

THE BIBLE AND JESUS

In order to lead boys to a fulfilling Christian manhood, some work needs to be done on how to portray the Jesus of the Bible rather than the Jesus of Christmas songs or misleading mythology. You may need to help boys to reconsider several aspects of their assumptions about Jesus.

THE PHYSICAL IMAGE OF JESUS

Work with boys on their ideas about Jesus' physical appearance. Do they think he was tall and slim, wearing a long white robe, and sporting a fashionable beard and flowing blond hair? The image so often portrayed of Jesus is not of someone that most boys want to be like. His nature was and is undeniably kind and compassionate, but you may need to kill some myths about his appearance.

- He would have had dark skin, dark hair and facial hair.

- His clothes would not have been spotlessly clean, as he walked from place to place in a dusty and hot land.

- Travelling on foot with his disciples, Jesus and his 'gang' might have appeared a little menacing or intimidating.

- He is not described as looking any different from other men, and he didn't have a halo! As far as we know from scripture, Jesus was kind and compassionate, but didn't look 'soft'.

- Towards the end of his life, particularly when dragging his own cross up the hill where he was to be crucified, Jesus would have been sweating, bleeding and suffering as any man would in that situation.

- Jesus' death would have been a frightening and ugly sight, with no redeeming features.

JESUS AS A CHILD

There is very little in scripture to help us understand what Jesus was like as a child, yet many boys, at a young age, will form an image of the young Jesus that is as far from reality as possible. The traditional hymns and carols that we sing about him contain a huge amount of sweet and misleading nonsense. Try to explore some of these issues with the boys in your group.

- If possible, bring into the group a young baby, with its parent or carer. Talk with your group about their own baby brothers or sisters. Make a list of all the things babies do—for example, crying, feeding, drinking, wetting and filling nappies, laughing, being sick, and so on. Then ask the boys if they think Jesus was different and didn't do any of those things.

- How might Jesus and his family have been viewed by their community? Talk about the fact that Mary and Joseph were not married when the angel told Mary that she would have a baby, and that they settled in Nazareth some time after Jesus was born.

- At the age of twelve, Jesus stayed behind in the temple to learn more about God and to talk with the religious leaders (who should have known more than he did). His parents lost him and were worried, and here we see a family struggling with an extraordinary child (Luke 2:41–52).

- Spend a little time thinking about the skills that Jesus would have learned from Joseph as he grew up. Joseph was a skilled carpenter, and Jesus would have looked up to him, copied him, and learned skills from him, just as any boy would learn from a father or father-figure.

JESUS AND HIS BATTLE IN LIFE

To ensure that boys get a balanced view of biblical teaching and a true view of the Gospels, we shouldn't avoid teaching about the Sermon on the Mount and the Beatitudes, the intensely practical miracle of turning water into wine, or the moving scene of Lazarus being brought back to life. All the wisdom of Jesus' teaching and all the supernatural kindness of miracles and healings are important to consider. To fully engage boys with this story, though, we also need to introduce them to the idea that Jesus was fully divine and fully human, and that he fought with every inch of his humanity.

Here are a few key themes and events in the life of Jesus that reveal his strength. Consider teaching and studying some of these accounts or others that also reveal the nature of God as a man.

- **Temptation:** Look at the temptations that Jesus faced—the physical and emotional challenge of living without food in the desert for 40 days, and his rejection of physical comfort, food and power (Luke 4:1–13). Ask the boys about their strength to resist temptation.

- **Rejection at home:** Consider what it would have felt like for Jesus, God on earth, to have so much to say and yet to be rejected by the people that he grew up with. He probably made furniture for these people; they were the ones who should have known him best, yet they tried to push him off a cliff (Luke 4:14–30). How would it feel if the people who knew you and claimed to be your friends turned against you and tried to kill you?

- **Good work and words ignored:** Mark 2:23—3:6 and many other passages show powerful leaders trying to catch Jesus out. Rather than listening to and learning from him, they retreated into their own rules and regulations. Explore with the boys the anger and frustration that this must have stirred up in Jesus.

- **His attitudes to children:** At the time of the Gospels, children were not valued, and Jesus' disciples tried to keep them away from him. Jesus was indignant about this, and rebuked his disciples (Mark 10:13–16). He valued people and things that, at the time, were not valued at all. He turned traditions on their heads. What would it be like to do and say the opposite of what everyone else thought was right?

- **His authority questioned:** Jesus was and is the Son of God, but he often faced people who thought they knew better than him, asking him what he thought he was doing and challenging his words and actions (for example, Luke

20). What would it be like to endure all of that criticism without being rude in return?

- **Anger at deception and misuse:** Jesus got angry when he saw how people were using the worship area of the temple as a place for liars and thieves to take people's money, so he turned the tables over. Children shouted praise to him, while the adults got angry and even more determined to get him killed (Matthew 21:12–17). What things do you see in the world or in your own life that make you angry because they are unfair or unjust?

THE TRUTH OF JESUS' DEATH FOR US

The 2004 film *The Passion of the Christ* showed a very graphic representation of the death of Jesus, with plenty of pain and horror in the scenes. Many Christians struggled to relate to this portrayal, perhaps having not fully considered the pain that a fully human incarnate Christ must have gone through. For boys, that reality will help them to consider Christ's true sacrifice. We don't want to scare boys into believing and trusting in Christ, but nor do we want them to drift away because they get the idea that there is no challenge in Christianity or their hero and leader didn't really suffer. Boys are helped by understanding the battles that Jesus fought, the tension he carried to the cross, the way he swam against the tide, his bravery and heroism, and the blood he shed.

- Help boys to understand the challenge that Jesus faced, knowing that, throughout the time when he was healing people, speaking wisdom and challenging the authorities, he was walking towards a painful death.

- Talk about Jesus' frustration as he continued to show that he really was the Son of God, but his disciples didn't understand.

- Consider the deep sense of betrayal and pain that Jesus would have felt on the night before his death—how he prayed not to have to go through with it, but also found the amazing courage to step forward and do what he had come to earth to do, to die and rise again.

- Focus a little on the punishment that Jesus received at the hands of the soldiers after his arrest, including the mockery, whipping, spitting and taunting, and the long thorns on the 'crown' that they made for him. Try to help the boys understand what it would have been like for Jesus, knowing he had the power to stop it all in an instant, to go through with it.

- Describe something of the politics involved. The Jewish religious leaders didn't like Jesus because he spoke wisdom and threatened their authority, and the Romans didn't want to risk a riot breaking out. So in the end no one was willing to fight for Jesus, and even those who had called his name in joy were now calling for him to be killed by being nailed to a cross.

- Share some of the reality of crucifixion, making your description age-appropriate but also honest. Explain a little about the pain involved, and the gradual and frightening sense of suffocation.

Boys need to know that the Jesus whom we love and serve was not a wimp but a strong man of action, who took massive risks and suffered intolerable punishments. This picture needs to be balanced with the compassionate, sensitive qualities that we also see in the Gospels: Jesus was countercultural in caring for the prostitute as well as in tipping over the tables in the temple. Boys need to be aware of this, so that when we ask them to live countercultural lives, they are able to relate to our Messiah in that way. Only then will boys stick with the church and grow up into godly men.

CHAPTER 8

ACTIVITIES WITH BOYS

We already know that boys like short tasks and challenges, enjoy hands-on activity, and learn by doing. We are also aware that, in many areas of life outside the church, boys have a powerful part to play in controlling what happens, whether by pester power and manipulation of their parents and carers at home, or as part of class and school councils. Boys really enjoy being involved, yet the church often expects them to be passive and inactive. This goes against their very nature, and is one of the many ways in which the church says to boys, 'This is not a place for you. You are not welcome here.'

SESSIONS JUST FOR THE BOYS?

Churches should be places where different backgrounds, ages and genders are together and learn to coexist for much of the time. The church has a significant role to play in encouraging the value of and respect for difference, and I believe it has a prophetic role in modelling how people of all backgrounds, ages and sexes can thrive, worship and enjoy being together. All-age or intergenerational worship is just one example; in children's groups and clubs and uniformed organisations, boys and girls can communicate, have fun, discuss and enjoy worthwhile times together. It is therefore important to make sure that the children's and young people's groups are not always strictly divided on gender lines.

It is increasingly controversial to suggest that boys need sessions and activities that are different from those for girls, but, as we considered earlier, girls can benefit from sessions just for them too. We have already seen that boys do need activities that are not always on offer in the mixed-gender groups that most of them attend. Uniformed organisations provide the chance for girls to be girls, but, in the main, do not offer the same for boys.

The issue is not only about activities and programmes; it is also about the way boys relax and interact in each other's company, which may not be so easy for them if girls are present. When boys spend time in a group without girls, they get to know each other better. There is no need for them to show off to girls, so they are more free to be themselves without feeling threatened by the other males. That sense of security and self-confidence becomes increasingly important as boys grow older. Therefore, churches should be thinking about how and when it may be appropriate to run some sessions for boys only. With careful work and sensitive management, a pattern could develop that suits all children, as well as the leaders.

Whether you meet with your children on a Sunday morning during the main service or at another time, you could provide some activities that are specifically boy- or girl-friendly as part of the main session. This would need to be done carefully, with some flexibility. Occasionally you may choose to provide an entirely different experience for the boys and the girls, splitting off as soon as you meet or come out of church worship, and offering alternative activities designed to appeal to different genders.

You could decide to have boys and girls meeting at different times. Girls may enjoy a pamper or make-up evening, even with their mums, while boys may prefer a games session with some men around. It shows a real commitment to our children of both genders if we are willing to put on extra events that are designed especially to make them feel at home.

If you have a group of children composed almost entirely of girls, you will need to work harder at providing content that will appeal to boys, and will need to ensure that you have at least one male leader to relate to that small number of boys. In order to hold on to your boys in this situation, it is really important to provide activities outside the group and a chance to meet up with other boys who 'do' church.

Leaders offering boys' activities in a mixed session or special events for boys should take into consideration the key times when boys are exposed to new peer groups, and when they face significant challenges of change. These will include the times when children change schools. As we have discussed, puberty affects the confidence of boys, and this is a time when, more than ever, boys need a male peer group with whom to bond as a loyal and supportive unit. Therefore, the church needs to consider how it can actively help children through that key transition, in order to bridge the gap, and also how it can make sure that the male peer group survives.

Once boys start puberty, there are many reasons why they don't want to be with girls so much, and they will come under significant social and peer pressure to leave your church if they don't have the support and encouragement of a peer group around them. If just one or two boys are left in the group at this point, they will almost certainly drift away unless a herculean effort is made to involve them in the life of the church.

In this situation, rather than clinging on to that boy, children's workers may need to think about where else he might go in order to find spiritual support, a male peer group, and good youth work that will keep him in the Christian faith. This can be a real sacrifice for churches and loyal, committed workers who have tried hard to provide for all their children, but we need to focus on the wider kingdom of God and not our own work. Helping these one or two boys to settle into the right place to grow may mean finding out when and where a youth group in another church meets, accompanying the boys to it and introducing them to the leaders there. It may even mean that the current leader needs to offer his services to that other church.

THE TIMING OF MEETINGS

The traditional time for church groups to meet is, of course, Sunday mornings. Children's groups generally operate alongside the 'adult' church, so families attend together but spend little if any time worshipping and learning together at church.

The gradual decline in Sunday morning church attendance has been encouraged by social and community factors that affect the nature of Sunday mornings for many families. For example, Sunday is family time. With changes in working patterns, many families now see Sunday as the *only* time when they can do things together, and the things they want to do together may not include church. Sunday is also 'free' time. This is the day when older relatives are visited, the home is cleaned and the washing done, or the food for the next week is purchased. Those necessary activities have to be done at some point, and Sunday may be the only time available.

Even if your church is doing a great job with children and attracts many boys, it's important to remember that some children don't have a choice about what they do on a Sunday. Even if they wanted to come to the group, their parents or carers may not allow them to, or may insist that they do other things instead.

Whether we like it or not, Sundays are no longer a time when everything stops. Once, people had very limited options for things to do on a Sunday, but now there are lots of alternatives. Families can go out for the day to an attraction just as easily on a Sunday as any other day. Sundays are therefore busy for children.

Boys may face a particular problem, given the popularity of Sunday morning football, cricket and rugby training and local league games. Of course, there are other options for girls too, but many parents of boys, and no parents of girls, have asked to discuss this problem with me. Many Christian parents face the challenging dilemma of whether to let their sons develop their skills and participate in healthy sports, or to stop them doing these activities, insisting that they go to church instead. The risk is that boys who are forced to do something they don't want to do will rebel and drop out of church activities as soon as they can.

We will consider church-based sporting options later, but every church that wants to reach children, and particularly boys, needs to consider whether a Sunday morning meeting time is ever going to be appropriate. We may need to think much more realistically and creatively about how and when we provide activities and sessions for boys.

That said, there are always exceptions. Some boys are so well connected with their peer group at church, and feel so much part of the worshipping community, that they still want to go to church on a Sunday morning, despite the alternative options. This may be partly because their family unit lives and breathes its faith every day, so the boys growing up in that environment don't see anything strange about going to church and would never consider other activities.

Some churches across the social spectrum have managed to keep Sunday morning groups thriving. When this happens, the essential ingredients always include a fully supportive church leadership, lively and active children's group leaders, men in children's ministry roles, and a programme that meets the needs of all who attend, not just the girls.

However, to meet the needs of children who don't have the option to attend on Sunday morning or who choose to do other things, churches need to invest more in children's ministry, provide more leaders, and deliver programmes and activities at different times and on different days. If we slavishly stick to Sunday morning only, we will not attract boys and we will risk losing those who do attend.

Giving boys responsibility

We need to consider what roles of responsibility we can give boys at church, in order to keep them engaged—beyond handing out hymn books. For example, boys may be good at operating the PA system or data projector. They may also be able to lead prayers if given freedom to do it creatively, to speak, or to play in the music group.

Train and encourage a small group of boys to work with those who run the technology of the church—the visual projection and sound system—learning how the system works and having a go at running it themselves, with careful oversight. This not only gives them new skills but also provides a mentoring relationship between the boys and the adults working with them, along with the sense of group bonding that boys need. Once they are trained, they could be included on the regular rota, thus making them feel that they have a role and investment in the church and church community. It also shows the wider church community that boys have something to offer. Many boys have been helped through church into adulthood by being given a role in the more technical aspects of church life.

You could form a worship band with boys who have musical ability. Start when the boys are young and develop the group as they develop their skills. There is a special bond in playing music together, and the band can quickly form into a good, supportive and loyal peer group. It may take some time to develop, but, again, it will give the boys a sense of purpose and responsibility, as well as providing adult mentors for them to work with and look up to.

Many churches reserve worship leading for senior, mature, sensible adults. As boys develop their musical skills in a group or band, one or two may be identified with the potential to lead worship. It is very difficult to stand up at the front of church to lead worship, so any potential should be carefully nurtured and developed, perhaps encouraging the young worship leader to lead a short time of praise with the children's groups first. There may come a time when the boy feels that he has the confidence to lead some worship for the whole church congregation. The sense of achievement and belonging among the boys will be significant if their abilities can be developed to this extent.

In churches that follow a more traditional style of worship, there are formal or ceremonial roles that boys can be encouraged to take on, which, again, will provide the positive mentoring and sense of purpose that boys require.

Invite older boys to work with younger ones in church activities, perhaps for a short period each week. This could mean, for example, preparing different boys to do some interactive prayers, lead a game, tell a Bible story or introduce the theme. Many boys will appreciate the opportunity to contribute something rather than being on the receiving end. The younger boys will be encouraged by seeing older boys in church and will view them as role models, while the boys who help out will be kept busy, gaining credibility and learning faith at the same time. Many of them will enjoy the experience and will benefit from being seen as good examples by the younger children. They will also experience the reality that children's work is not always easy but is something that men can do as well as women. This may encourage them to consider working in children's ministry when they grow into men. If you give them these opportunities, remember that it will also be necessary to provide alternative times for teaching, learning and worship for the older boys.

Forming a 'boys' council' is a way of helping boys to take some responsibility in commenting on and shaping the planning and delivery of their activities and programmes. The council should give boys the opportunity to say what they would like to do within church children's work and in the wider church community. It not only gives them an important voice, but it also reinforces the message that boys are important to the church and that you want to hear what they have to say.

Remember that boys enjoy working with men. Encourage

them to help with church working parties, doing practical things around the church, such as land clearance, decorating, woodwork or rubbish disposal. Some of these activities may not seem immediately attractive, but, with the addition of some bacon sandwiches, they can help boys to engage with the men of the church.

Who Let The Dads Out? is a BRF initiative aimed at encouraging dads to spend time with their young children (see www.wholetthedadsout.org.uk). Typically, sessions run in church premises on Saturday mornings, with games and activities for the children, and food and chat for the dads with men from the church. Boys who attend as participants will be younger children with their fathers or male carers. However, there is a role for older boys in helping the men from church to set up the room, run the activities and support the children who are playing there. Boys will benefit from being in a church environment where men are taking the lead and having a worthwhile role to play.

ACTIVITIES IN CHILDREN'S GROUPS

Boys appreciate opportunities to let off steam and use up some of their energy, yet many of the activities, programmes and syllabuses available for children's work do not include much in the way of physical activity. This is compounded by the reality that, in many churches, children's work takes place in small, cramped spaces, or there is a pressure to be quiet in order to avoid disturbing the adult worship. Those practical hindrances are difficult to change quickly, but the fact is that boys will not thrive if they are cooped up and expected to be quiet all the time.

Consider how you can build in some space for boys (and girls if they wish) to meet before church begins, to play a few games and let off steam. It could be as simple as a kick-around on nearby grass, a running relay around the church, or simple throw-and-catch games.

Many boys enjoy watching and participating in football, and will be used to showing their support for a team with chants and repeated phrases. Work with the group on a simple chant or phrase that can be shouted out at the beginning of the children's group session, as the boys gather before church, as they leave to go home, or during the session, even if it does briefly interrupt the adults. The opportunity to make some noise is especially beneficial if the children have been kept in church for a while and have had to be quiet and behave in a controlled way. It gives boys the chance to be noisy and free, and helps them to form the important sense of group identity that they both enjoy and need.

If possible, start each session with a simple physical game or stretching exercise. This can be done quietly, and doesn't have to last too long. Here are some suggestions.

- **Touch the wall:** The leader simply says 'Far', 'Near', 'Left' or 'Right' to identify the wall that the children should run, walk or hop to. You could expand their biblical knowledge by naming the four walls after books in the Bible or Bible characters.

- **Head, shoulders, knees and toes:** Without singing the song (unless they and you want to), stand all the children in front of you and say each of the body parts in random order, with the children expected to touch them quickly.

To add a different twist, you could point to a part of your body that is different from the one you say. Alternatively, this activity could be done in pairs, with the boys gently touching the appropriate body part on each other.

- **Tag:** A simple game of tag, starting with a leader, can be a quick way to let off energy and can be done silently to add a little challenge and tension to the game.

- **Parachute games:** If you have a parachute or play canopy, it is worth using it for a few minutes regularly. Children, particularly boys, love playing simple parachute games over and over again, and most parachute games are simple, physical and tiring.

- **Leapfrog:** If there is enough space and the children in your group can play carefully and follow simple ground rules, an old-fashioned game of leapfrog, for a very limited time of two or three minutes, is enough to help boys let off steam and then calm themselves for quieter activities.

- **Softball touch:** Using a soft football, leaders at each end of the room roll the ball to catch the leg or foot of a child, who is then out of the game. This is gently competitive, physical, and can also be done silently if noise is likely to be an issue.

- **Gospel game:** Devise a simple movement for each of the names of the Gospels. For instance, 'Matthew' could be rowing a boat, 'Mark' jumping up and down, 'Luke' lying down on the floor, and 'John' doing star jumps.

- **Trust games:** Boys enjoy risk, and trust games offer them the opportunity to take risks, as well as developing a level of connection with each other. Start with a boy falling backwards with knees straight, being caught by a leader standing behind him. Then try having a pair of boys to catch the falling one. Make sure the leader is still there and ready to catch if anything goes wrong. Similarly, boys can learn to trust each other by having one blindfolded and led or guided by following verbal instructions given by someone else.

- **Exercises:** Some schools use a short period of brisk exercise at the start of the day to energise the pupils. Likewise, the boys in your church group will enjoy some simple jumping around or other movement to music. This activity could be led by an adult, and in turn by various children.

BOYS AND SWEATY CHURCH

Sweaty Church started in York and has grown with new examples across the UK and a resource website to help push it forward (https://sweatychurch.wordpress.com). Its initial goal was to find a much more active approach to Sunday worship, especially with boys in mind. Sweaty Church is not exclusively for boys, but the contents of each session include the active elements that boys value, and it is aimed at children aged seven to eleven and their families. Sweaty Church was developed by using the talents of members of the congregation in sport and activity, combining the use of the church with activities, sports and games on the field next to the building. Sweaty Church takes place on Sunday afternoons so that families who are busy with shopping, visiting and sports teams and activities in the morning can still attend and take part in worship, albeit in a style that is different from what takes place in the morning.

BOYS AND MESSY CHURCH

BRF's Messy Church (www.messychurch.org.uk) has become a key way for churches to gain and develop contact with families. Typically running once a month, Messy Church events have a focus on craft activities, plus time to gather for worship and enjoy food together. No Messy Church is exactly the same as another, and many are really good at adapting to meet the needs of their children and families.

One of the issues that Messy Church is addressing is how to continue to engage with boys. Not all boys enjoy doing craft activities, and they may not like to be confined to tables, doing the same thing as others. As in church children's work, boys can tend to stop attending and, in my experience, there are often fewer boys present than girls.

However, Messy Church provides lots of useful resources to support more active and creative ways to help boys remain involved. The books *Extreme Crafts for Messy Churches* and *Sports Fun for Messy Churches* both offer some really good suggestions to help Messy Church connect more with active boys who want to have more physical activity.

Again, bridging the gap for boys as they reach puberty is something that churches can help with. Boys like to take on responsibilities and, with proper supervision, there is no reason why boys can't be recruited to help alongside the adult team at Messy Church.

BOYS AND FOOD

If you want to attract boys to events, activities and clubs, it's a good idea to provide food as part of it. Most boys, particularly as they get older and adolescence kicks in, will appear to have endless appetites and will devour anything put in front of them. Here are some simple suggestions for food-based activities.

- **Snack time:** When boys get hungry, they can also be disruptive and difficult to handle. If the session is long enough and there's a need for it, provide very brief snacks for the boys between other activities. Make sure that, as far as possible, the food offered does not contain E numbers, and check with their parents for allergies.

- **Pizza evenings:** Times to eat pizza, play games and do a bit of Bible study or discussion about faith could be attractive to boys, and will help form the peer group that keeps them connected. A little bit of special attention is valued by boys and helps to make them feel cared for.

- **Moving meal:** Arrange for different people from the church community, within easy walking distance from each other, to provide a course each for all the boys. Meet at the first home, eat and discuss one topic or Bible story, then move on to the next home for a second course and the next discussion.

- **Boys' breakfast:** Provide breakfast occasionally on a Saturday and meet to eat, chat and develop sharing and peer group support. This could be an opportunity for a few men from the congregation to come along simply to get to know some of the boys.

- **Food and footy:** Gather at a home, have some food and chat, and play a Fifa or other console football game tournament, providing a small prize for the winner.

- **Boys' Bake Off:** Many boys enjoy cooking, as it is active and messy, and can end with a really good result. You could do some physical cooking that takes a bit of energy—for example, baking bread or cakes without the use of electric mixers or other labour-saving gadgets. This could be an opportunity for boys to connect with men in the congregation who have cooking and baking skills.

BOYS AND EVANGELISM

Over the past 30 years or so, there has been a move away from direct evangelism to children, towards an approach that meets the needs of children and families, such as Messy Church. These events draw people into the Christian world, even if the traditional inherited church doesn't see the fruit or recognise what God is doing.

Boys who are part of the church or on the fringes will have the confidence to invite their friends to any event with elements that are attractive to boys. However hard schools workers and church-based youth and children's workers try, by far the best evangelists to boys are other boys. Sport can be a draw, as can food. Any activity that provides something 'different', delivered by men for boys, will serve the purpose of attracting boys and helping them integrate into the peer group. As many of the theorists point out, 'belonging' usually comes before 'believing'. When boys are drawn in and start to engage with worship and teaching, then you can be a little more intentional about sharing what it means to be a Christian.

Sports and teams

Boys work out who they are, how they fit, and what being a boy means by being in peer groups with other boys. The church has recognised this in the past, through the founding and development of uniformed organisations that worked with boys, and through some other church-based activities. Sport is one of the key areas where boys can get actively involved with other boys and learn how to relate, how to follow rules, and how to be united in a common aim. This, along with the sense of risk and courage required to be fully committed, helps boys develop in a positive way.

Some of the most familiar and long-standing teams in English football history have clear links to church groups in their past. Everton and Aston Villa, to name but two, were set up for men and older boys in church congregations at a time when there was no such thing as a 'teenager'. So how can we encourage boys to form teams, be part of teams, and benefit from all that sporting unity can bring? The following suggestions may be helpful.

- Provide plenty of sport and physical activity that appeals to the energy, competitive nature and hands-on approach of boys.

- Provide a weekly or other regular opportunity for boys simply to have a football kick-around and play with others from the church.

- Consider joining with another church to do sports from time to time. Boys will benefit from being in larger groups, and will be reminded that going to church is something that other boys do too.

- Don't make everything competitive, but do remember that boys like competition and relish the opportunity to win, as well as needing to learn that they can't always be victorious.

- Start a group for boys from within and outside the church to learn football skills, using local Christian men who have the skills and are appropriately selected and checked. Provide it at a low cost and make it good fun, but don't be afraid to spend a few minutes talking about God and the Christian faith, either before you play or afterwards. Themes of following rules, being determined, feeling pain, working as a team, avoiding selfishness, fair play, grace, forgiveness and using the skills God has given us are all very relevant in helping boys connect their sport with their faith.

- Find out if there are any men in the church with general coaching skills who would be willing to lead occasional sessions with the boys in the group, whether they are particularly skilled or not in the sport involved.

CHURCH SPORTS TEAMS

Some local areas have church football leagues for men and for boys, and some local churches have football teams for boys that engage in competitions and leagues with other teams.

These teams generally play at other times than on Sunday mornings—but this may mean they are missing an opportunity. If your church is losing boys because they wish to do sports on a Sunday morning, it is worth considering whether you could set up a Sunday football team from the church. It might be feasible if you have enough suitable boys in your own church and can recruit more from among the friends of the boys who are connected with church, or by working with another local church. Once the team is established and developing, there could be a chance for it to play in a local Sunday morning league.

This could apply to a range of sports, including cricket and rugby, but I suspect that football is the most often played and watched of Sunday morning games. However, all sports have organisations and structures to help teams that are starting up, as well as clear guidelines and procedures to help keep children safe.

For a church to develop a team to play in a Sunday league is not quite as opposed to church and faith development as it might sound. Church should be in the world with the people. We know that life continues in our communities on a Sunday morning, despite the protestations of the church over the last few decades of rapid change. By setting up Sunday sports teams, we can take our place out there in the world, showing that church is accessible and flexible and understands the real world. The church is, in a sense, in a 'marketplace' for the attention and commitment of boys. With regard to boys who have sporting ability, we will never succeed in dragging them away from an activity they love, so we need to think more creatively about how we can keep alive their connection and relationship with the church.

Boys' teams can be a real witness to Christ on the sports field. Of course, boys will try to win and may not always behave or respond perfectly, with pure motives, in the middle of a game. With the right training, however, their discipline, response to others and sportsmanship can be a witness to the other teams and spectators.

You may decide that all who want to be in the team

need to agree to some degree of Christian input. This could involve a discussion of aspects of faith after the match for 30 minutes, for 15 minutes during a training session, or at an entirely separate time and place. You could explore further some of the themes mentioned above, and provide some more activities that boys will enjoy doing.

When they participate in sports linked with the church, boys will be connecting with men and seeing role models of dedication and commitment that are really helpful. The majority of boys enjoy sport as a pastime to watch and to take part in. Churches can help a great deal by taking this enjoyment seriously and working out how they can connect church with sport.

CHAPTER 9

MENTORING AND SUPPORTING BOYS

BOYS NEED BOYS

We know that the peer group is really important to young people, and a peer group that is developing in the Christian faith and wants to know more about God is potentially hugely significant for the church. We want the boys we work with to take their faith into the wider world with them, and also to care for their peers out there as well as in their church-based groups. Boys need encouragement to look out for each other, to meet up, and to be as open about their faith as they can be in school and in their community. There is real strength in numbers, and they will show dedication to each other and spur each other on to do more, learn more and speak out for Christ more. Those strong friendships and the kindred spirit that can develop between boys often prove to be very significant, powerful and enduring. Boys can become men together and continue to support each other through the tough challenges of the adult Christian life.

BOYS NEED MEN

The role models provided by Christian men play a significant part in the way boys see themselves and their futures. Boys are not fully formed at birth. They grow slowly, physically and emotionally; they learn as they go along, through risk and experience, and they gradually discern what a 'man' is. With the right support at home and in church, they are formed into the men that God wants them to be, and they look to others to set them the right example. In order to understand what it means to be a credible Christian man, they need it to be demonstrated by credible Christian men.

Churches need to work with parents in bringing up their boys. There are many books and parenting websites available to help with the issues that parents and carers encounter. In a church context we also need to understand that boys can often be a handful and a challenge, but they are made in the image of God, and God doesn't make mistakes.

In particular, we can help parents and carers with discipline. Many of the suggestions in this book about managing behaviour in church would work just as well in the home, and, while boys do need the space to be boys and be exuberant, they also need to know when it's right to conform and where the boundaries are drawn. There are many reasons why parents struggle to say 'no' to their children, and this is not the place to explore those issues, but boys do need to learn that, in reality, they can't always have and do whatever they like.

Parents also need to work with the church to help boys in their faith development. If worship, prayer and faith activities are carried out in the home, this helps to develop essential habits for boys.

However, it's important to remember that dads are not always the best example for boys. The reality is that not all boys have a dad at home, and, for some, the positive Christian role model that they are searching for is not to be found in the man who lives at home. In any case, boys may not always relate well to their dads. As they get older, some boys develop power and territory issues with their dads, and they fight over who is in charge. This is natural as the boy moves toward manhood and tests out the strength of his own parent, but it can be a very difficult phase in the teenage years.

Challenge your church to consider what it would be like if all the boys left, and no men were there in the future. Ask the church to consider releasing men from other jobs and leadership roles to work with children as role models for boys. This could mean the male church leaders taking their turn on a rota and joining in with the children's groups on a regular basis. It could also mean that the church considers its priorities more carefully, to find the right people for the right roles. As you work through this issue, remind your church that in most other areas of boys' lives, including sports, schools and community groups, the need for male leaders is readily accepted.

MEN IN THE BACKGROUND

There are many ways that men in the church can be involved and show a good example to boys without having to take on the deeper and more significant role of leading children's ministry. Much of this involvement happens naturally in some churches, and can be encouraged with only a little intentional thinking.

You could set up an informal link scheme between appropriate men and boys in the congregation. The men would be responsible for chatting to the boys at the end of a service, finding out how they're doing, then praying about those things during the week and asking again about them at the next opportunity. Safeguarding must be considered, of course. All conversations should take place in public, with parents and carers keeping an eye on their boys and taking some responsibility, and any adults known to be inappropriate should not be part of the informal pairings.

It may also be possible to link boys in with men's ministry. Many churches have set up ministry especially for men, including quiz nights, discussions, sports activities or events, breakfast together on the occasional Saturday, curry nights at the local restaurant, and so on. My experience of these groups is that they exist to encourage and nurture the men who attend, and as a gentle form of evangelism, providing an opportunity to invite friends along. It would not necessarily be appropriate for all men's groups to be open to boys, but there may be times when boys of a certain age or maturity in the church can be invited to join in. The benefits are numerous. Those boys will feel that they have been noticed and are seen as part of the body of the church. They will sense that they are growing up and being respected by the men of the church. They will also see that the church is a place for men as well as women, and therefore a place for boys as well as girls.

Many men and boys will enjoy weekends away together, perhaps camping, doing lots of activities and having some times of worship and teaching. It may seem like a daunting challenge to organise such events, but it will have a significant impact on boys to see their own dads or other men living a true and real faith while enjoying doing other active things together. Of course, not all dads would be able or willing to come, or they may not be connected or live in the home with their sons. These situations need to be handled carefully, but with some sensitivity it could be possible for other men to act as 'dads' for the weekend and form good mentoring relationships.

In your church groups, have a regular slot—perhaps monthly or each half term—where you invite a male guest to meet the boys and answer questions. Interview the guest, or ask the children to prepare questions for them in advance if the prospect of being put on the spot is a little daunting for them. The more help you can give, the better. The type of people you might invite could include the following:

- A teenager who has had some success in sport or music.

- Young men from the church who have recently gone to university, to talk about the challenges of moving away from home and God's care for them.

- Men who have been called by God to do their work, whether in a Christian faith setting or in the secular world. Let them explain not only what they do but also their sense of God's call to that work, and what difference they feel they can make in the world as a Christian. This will help boys to think about what God might want them to do in their adult lives.

- Men who have particular skills, hobbies and interests that the boys will appreciate learning about. Allowing a man to talk a little, demonstrate their skills and answer questions is a low-key way for boys to see that Christian men are real, and that the church is a place for both men and boys.

- Men who are doing mission work abroad. Let them share with the boys some of the challenges and battles that mission workers face, and the courage and determination that they have to have, based on their faith in Christ.

MEN AS LEADERS

Do try to find more men to work with the children's and youth teams in your church. I know this is not nearly as easy as it sounds, and there are issues of time and energy to be addressed before most men will volunteer. There are also many myths surrounding children's work, which need to be dispelled before the church can hope to achieve a positive gender balance and great role models for boys. Here are some of the flawed statements that you might have heard.

- 'Women, not men, should work with children.' It is now understood that, while many women have a natural ability to 'nurture', men also have a role to play in children's development. Children's ministry is not 'women's work', and it should never be seen as 'child-minding'.

- 'Children won't be safe if men are around.' This is an insult to the men who have had long and fruitful ministries with children. Most men do not want to harm children; there is a tiny minority of men—and women—who do. With proper recruitment and good practice, children will be safe and happy, and will benefit a great deal from having men to work with them.

- 'Children's work is not important enough for men.' Can there be anything more 'important' than helping young lives develop and opening the minds of children to the gifts that God has to offer? There may be men in your church who have other roles, but would love to work with children if they could.

- 'Children's work is about being silly!' There are many ways to communicate the gospel: children learn through fun, through stories, through activities, through quiet times and through reflection. Boys learn particularly well from activities and from male role models. Most people who work with children not only have fun, but learn from the children too.

If there are men who have suitable gifts to offer and could make a huge difference to boys in the church, we need to ask them some questions:

- Could God be calling you out of your current church work to this important ministry?

- Do you want to see a church where women and men are equal in numbers, and where there are plenty of boys and young men to take on responsibilities?

- Could you go along to some children's activities in your church and see what happens?

- Could you offer just to be around for boys to see and talk to, so that they have contact with an example of a male Christian?

- Could you contribute to planning sessions so that the needs of boys are considered?

Even when they are working with boys, some men find it difficult to be authentic in that role. If the programme and materials used tend to be more attractive to girls, and if all the other leaders are female, it can be hard for the male leader to be different. Many men will conform to the team's overall approach and will be unwilling or unable to reveal their own spiritual lives to the boys. So men who work as children's group leaders with boys need to have certain qualities.

First, they need to be willing to give the necessary time to the work. We live in a 'cash-rich but time-poor' world, and many adults face increasing pressures in their work lives. In churches, as attendance reduces and congregations grow older, the few who are willing to do things end up with even more jobs to do. Even retired men may be busy with volunteering and other responsibilities. Men who work with boys need to be committed to the work and give it the dedication it requires, and that may mean giving up other things.

Men who work with boys need to offer a model of strength. Boys can relate to struggle, fight, determination and energetic vision, and they model themselves on what they see in adults. Male children's workers should therefore be able to talk openly and without embarrassment about what they believe and what being a Christian means to them. They need to have the confidence to share how they pray, what God does for them, and how faith in Jesus helps them.

However, they also need to be realistic and vulnerable. Boys are looking for strong role models, but they also need to accept that being a man is about having failings and problems too. Children see through insincere people and have a great deal of respect for those who are honest.

Men working with children are, of course, needed to set rooms up, take the lead, tell stories, answer questions, and do all the other jobs that come with the territory. However, most children remember far more about what we do and what we are like as people than about what we say. Men who are capable and gifted, spiritual and down-to-earth at the same time, and who care about helping boys, will have a huge impact.

Mentoring boys

If boys are to grow with guidance from older teens and adult men, it may be helpful to set up a mentoring arrangement in which each individual is linked up with one adult and meets with him regularly. Mentoring schemes are developing in both secular work and teenage Christian ministry, and, with the right boundaries and safeguarding considerations, they can have a powerful influence on young men. In children's groups, mentoring is less likely to be about one-to-one conversations and discussion, where the mentor and mentee discuss particular issues and challenges, as younger boys will find it too difficult and, in any case, are not facing the issues that arise with puberty.

Mentoring for boys could include the following.

- Give each male leader responsibility for looking out for certain boys—simply checking that they are well and that there aren't any problems in their lives, helping them if they get angry or upset or if they need to be disciplined, and being the main link with their parents and carers.

- Learn more about the whole boy, not just the one who presents at church! What is he interested in? What motivates and excites him? What is going on in his home or school life, that might be useful to know?

- Encourage older boys, including appropriately wise and mature teenagers, to get alongside boys and support those who have behavioural difficulties or particular needs.

- Provide some space and freedom in the programme so that boys who want to talk can approach a leader and have a personal conversation. If schedules are too full and busy, this sort of space is not available and boys may miss out on the opportunity to seek help and advice.

- Ensure that male leaders all set a good example of language and behaviour for boys to follow, participating fully in activities, helping with worship and prayer, and showing the boys that these are good things to do.

- Provide group mentoring, led by teenagers, for boys who are approaching the move from one school to another. This might simply be an opportunity for the teenage boys who have been through that transition to talk about what it is like, allowing the younger children to share some of their concerns.

- Set up longer-term mentoring for boys with particular problems. This could be a set period of four or six sessions, with the full knowledge and support of the parents or carers and in a place where interactions can be observed at all times. It could follow a bereavement or other trauma that has affected the boy, and may need to lead to professional counselling.

CHAPTER 10

CONTINUING WITH BOYS

We need to continue to work with boys as they become men.
If your church is able to get male leaders in place and provide
all the other opportunities for boys suggested so far, you will
stand more than an average chance of developing a peer
group of boys into their teens who feel that the church is a
place for them and that they have a role to play. The next
step, and the most challenging one, is to help them move
into manhood.

Of course, boys don't suddenly become men—although,
until the 'invention' of teenagers, boys were boys until
they went to work, and became men as they grew in the
adult environment. Many people feel that, with statutory
education in the UK being extended gradually to 18, boys
are remaining boys for longer and are finding it harder to
discover what manhood is and when it begins.

Perhaps the thing that is missing for boys is some form of
initiation into manhood. Christian teenagers need to have a
definite experience that enables them to step over from one
state to the other, just as much as non-Christians do.

SOCIAL AND SEXUAL INITIATION

In the majority of Western cultures, there is no clear stage
of initiation that marks out the point when a boy becomes

a man. We may consider the transition from primary to secondary school as significant, which it is, but it is not the great step forward that marks pupils aged 12 and 13 out as men, as anyone in teaching or younger youth work will tell you.

By contrast, other cultures have rituals and initiation rights that take boys into manhood. For instance, the Bar Mitzvah ceremony in the Jewish community (for both observant and cultural Jews) marks the stage when, at 13, a boy is considered old enough to take responsibility for his own actions and to learn and follow the Jewish laws. These ceremonies are often marked with lavish parties and gifts, usually of cash. Tribal cultures have rituals that involve sending boys into the desert or jungle to fend for themselves for a period before returning to the tribe and being recognised as men.

The reality for many boys in our communities is that they mark their step from childhood to manhood by doing 'adult' things. For some, this step will be the first time they drink too much alcohol or take drugs. For many, it will be the move into sexual activity, which raises a whole load of issues about relationships, responsibility, the use of pornography and attitudes to girls and women. Even when boys have moved through these social and sexual types of initiation, our society keeps them in school with little opportunity to take up the responsibilities of adult men.

CHRISTIAN INITIATION

We don't want the boys we work with in churches to see having sex or getting drunk as the best or only way to step into manhood. Yet there are few markers, if any, to help

Christian boys develop and find their established place in the adult family of the church.

Some churches may insist on adult baptism as a rite of passage; for some boys, this can be a significant step forward, as some denominations link adult responsibilities and church membership with baptism. There is certainly something important for a boy about standing up in public and declaring his faith as he moves toward adulthood.

The Church of England sees confirmation as a significant step toward adulthood, although the significance is lessened if boys are confirmed at the age of eleven or twelve. In any case, is the moment when a bishop in strange clothing places his or her hands on the boy's head really experienced as a major staging post on the journey to being a man? Despite the fact that, like believer's or adult baptism, confirmation provides a useful opportunity for the boy to declare his faith in public, taking on personally the vows made for him when baptised as a baby or child, I am yet to be convinced that, for most boys, it makes a huge difference. Many men speak of having had little choice in their experience of confirmation. Some even describe it as a 'passing out parade', after which church became an aspect of their childhood past rather than their adult future.

Churches need to take on some responsibility for placing barriers in the way of boys' spiritual growth and progress. We set arbitrary age limits for when children can fully take part or have a role to play, and we indulge in theological point-scoring about whether a child or teenager fully understands concepts that are, by definition, mysteries of God's grace. So the church needs to take a few steps in order to help boys make the transition, and we might start by asking some questions.

Consider the 'staging posts' built into the structures of your children's and youth work. Do the boys and their parents understand those points along the journey? Do teenage boys know what it means to be seen as an adult in the church? Does the church make enough of teenagers who are growing into men, celebrating their physical and spiritual growth?

Look at the official or normally accepted rites of passage in your church, which are likely to follow the traditional pattern of baptism at some stage and possibly confirmation. Some churches have found that, for both boys and girls, allowing children to receive Communion before taking the step of confirmation or believer's or adult baptism can provide them with a useful staging post, giving an opportunity for children to learn again the basics of Christianity and make a public declaration of their faith. This acknowledges that they are on a journey of faith, and that the journey continues into adulthood.

Work on developing a list of some of the basic elements that your church wants to teach young men. Then compare those principles with the teaching that the young people generally receive, and see what needs to be added to provide a more structured and helpful aid to learning.

Provide some direct and appropriately targeted teaching for boys on what it means to be a Christian man. There are published materials available for young people in general, and now a few are specifically aimed at teenage boys. One of these, called *ManMade* and subtitled 'A rites of passage course for teenage guys', is written by Darren Quinnell and produced by a consortium of agencies including Christian Vision for Men, Urban Saints and The Boys' Brigade. It provides session outlines, ideas for outdoor and challenge activities, and a DVD of extra resources.

Alternatively, a simple set of four ideas and themes is given below.

GOD'S MEN

Here are four basic areas to discuss and explore with the boys in a youth group. Bible stories and passages are suggested, along with questions to share and talk through.

GOD'S MEN: DARING

To be daring means to take risks, despite the possible consequences. Think of David, the young shepherd who felt that God had called him to dare to stand against the giant Philistine warrior, Goliath. David happened to be very skilled with a sling and stone, and won the battle (see 1 Samuel 17). To be daring is about taking a brave step forward and trusting God for the consequences.

Christian men are daring. What sort of behaviour would be seen as daring with your friends and other men at school, college or work? Is it daring to avoid dirty jokes and not use bad language? How far would you dare to go in standing up for what you believe?

GOD'S MEN: DETERMINED

To be determined means seeing things through to the end, and not giving up. The first apostles were the church leaders of their time, but they did not have much support, and the threat of arrest and death was always with them. Paul and Peter, between them, suffered accusations, arrest, imprisonment, tough questioning, and shipwreck. They continued despite all of those obstacles, determined to share the message of Jesus.

Christian men are determined. What are you determined to do? Are you really determined to see others know about

Jesus, and to help them find out more? If you face trouble for being a Christian, will you be determined to stand firm?

GOD'S MEN: DRIVEN

To be driven means to have a vision and to go all out to see it happen. Nehemiah was concerned that the walls of Jerusalem were in ruins, and he prayed to God for help. Nehemiah knew that it was his job to get the walls rebuilt, and he was passionate about it, defeating enemies who tried to stop him and organising all the work (Nehemiah 1—6).

God's men are driven by a vision and passion to do God's work. What motivates you and gets you excited? What drives you and gives you a vision for the future? If God gave you a clear vision, would you drive it through?

GOD'S MEN: DIFFERENT

To be different means not going along with the crowd. Jesus is the ultimate example of a man, fully human, who was different from all others. We read in the Gospels that he had the strength to survive persecution, temptation and even death, and the compassion to bring healing and hope to all people. People wanted to know more about him simply because he was not the same as anyone else.

God's men are different in the things they do and the way they behave. How easy is it to be different from the crowd? How different from other young men do you think you are? How could you be so different that people wanted to know more about your faith, and more about Jesus?

CELEBRATING CHRISTIAN MANHOOD

Your church may want to provide a carefully planned and delivered process of transition or initiation for boys and young men at some point during their teenage years. This could be done annually or less often, depending on the number of teenage boys in the church.

- Provide a course of consistent and helpful teaching on what it means to be a man of God, and the costs and challenges involved.

- Take the 15- to 16-year-old boys away together to engage in a mixture of worship, teaching, activities, outdoor pursuits and games. The event should include a clear and unambiguous appeal to them to move on from boyhood to Christian manhood, recommitting their lives to Christ.

- While you are away, help each boy to identify one thing he can do in and for the church that would mark his transition from a boy to a man. It should be related to the particular skills of the young man concerned, and might include giving a teenager the opportunity to preach, allowing him to lead some worship, or recognising a significant ministry that he could offer in other areas of church life.

- After the time away, give each boy the opportunity to do the one thing he has identified. Ensure that his significant contribution is noted and marked by the church.

- Hold a celebration service for all the boys and young men in the church, focusing on the cohort who have gone through the initiation process. The service could include some of their contributions, some testimony about what God is teaching them and how they want to live in the future, and prayer for them as they step forward into Christian manhood.

- Give the boys something significant and important as a gift. They will already have a Bible, and the gift doesn't necessarily need to have spiritual value. The important point is that it should be carefully chosen and specific to each boy, so that the gift is memorable for them.

- Continue the theme of celebration after the service with food and a party atmosphere, ensuring that the young men who have been through the process have a sense of purpose and responsibility as men of God.

- Work with this group of young men on how they can contribute to church life and serve the church community more in future, taking on more responsibility as Christian men.

Once boys reach Christian manhood, they need to be in a church that values them and recognises that men, as well as boys, are different and need different things. This remains a problem, and many men have given up on church and abandoned their faith because the church doesn't provide the appropriate foundations and opportunities for them to thrive and grow. Many of the suggestions in this book for encouraging boys will be helpful to men too. Ultimately, though, the way forward for men and the church is a whole different issue.

Conclusion

What are boys and men looking for? David Murrow, in his book *Why Men Hate Going to Church*, explores what men are searching for in the activities they take part in and commit to. Boys are searching for similar inspiration and will not commit to becoming men of Christ if they don't find it in the church. Here are some of the things that boys are seeking:

- They are looking for success.

- They are looking for a heroic figure.

- They are looking for a leader they want to follow.

- They are looking for something to do.

- They are looking for a vision to motivate them.

The needs on this list can be met to an extent in our churches, but we may not yet clearly understand that, to keep boys, many churches need to change both radically and quickly. We may be asking ourselves how we have managed to keep any boys in our churches to this point. Many of those who are there, by the grace of God, have learned to endure inappropriate teaching and inadequate support. They may have simply been told that 'that's what we do' as a family and have accepted that they have little choice but to go along with it.

All is not lost, however, and, while the ideas and suggestions in this book will not all work in every situation, they do aim to bring something to the table. In summary, this is what we must try to do:

- Remember that boys and girls are different.

- Don't pressurise boys to conform too much.

- Think through the particular needs that boys have.

- Make sure that boys in church have something to do, see and say.

- Consider how 'boy-friendly' our teaching and resource materials are.

- Encourage more men to work with boys.

- Help boys to develop their peer group.

- Provide significant male role models.

- Give boys a vision and a purpose.

- Help boys over transitions and into manhood.

FURTHER THINKING AND READING

There are countless reports and strategies to raise the educational achievement of boys, and many other books that study what makes boys tick and what influences can be damaging to them. These books have helped me think around the issue and have provided some detailed analysis that you may wish to explore in more depth. I've included three titles of my own that might help too. Most are still in print and should be easily accessible.

- Steve Biddulph, *Raising Boys* (Harper Thorsons, 2015)

- Francis Bridger, *Children Finding Faith* (SU, 2000)

- Peter Brierley, *Reaching and Keeping Tweenagers* (Christian Research, 2002)

- Kathryn Copsey, *From the Ground Up* (Kindle edition by Amazon Media, 2013)

- John Eldredge, *Wild at Heart* (John Eldredge, 2011)

- Penny Frank, *Every Child a Chance to Choose* (Kingsway, 2002)

- Stephen Frost, Ann Phoenix and Rob Pattman, *Young Masculinities* (Palgrave, 2002)

- Nick Harding, *Bible Heroes* (SU, 2011)

- Nick Harding, *Boys, God and the Church* (Grove, 2007)

- Nick Harding, *Kids' Culture* (SU, 2003)

- David Hay and Rebecca Nye, *The Spirit of the Child* (Jessica Kingsley, 2006)

- Roy McCloughry, *Hearing Men's Voices* (Hodder and Stoughton, 1999)

- Roy McCloughry, *Men and Masculinity* (Hodder and Stoughton, 1992)

- David Murrow, *Why Men Hate Going to Church* (David Murrow, 2011)

- Darren Quinnell, *ManMade* (Emerging Culture, 2010)

- Leonard Sax, *Boys Adrift* (Basic Books, 2009)

- Sami Timimi, *Naughty Boys* (Palgrave Macmillan, 2005)

- Richard Witham, *Top Tips Working with Lads* (SU, 2011)

- Philip Zimbardo and Nikita D. Coulombe, *Man Disconnected* (Rider, 2016)

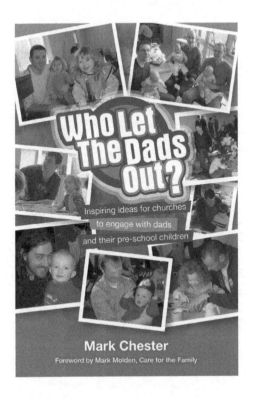

This book tells the story of how Who Let The Dads Out? came into being. It gives a practical guide for setting up and running the monthly sessions, complete with theological background, real-life case studies, helpful hints and tips, and twelve easy craft ideas.

Who Let The Dads Out?
Inspiring ideas for churches to engage with dads and their pre-school children
Mark Chester
978 1 84101 885 0   £6.99

brfonline.org.uk